ILLEGAL GUNS IN THE WRONG HANDS

Patterns of Gun Acquisition and Use Among Serious Juvenile Delinquents

David C. May
G. Roger Jarjoura

University Press of America,® Inc.
Lanham · Boulder · New York · Toronto · Oxford

Copyright © 2006 by
University Press of America,® Inc.
4501 Forbes Boulevard
Suite 200
Lanham, Maryland 20706
UPA Acquisitions Department (301) 459-3366

PO Box 317
Oxford
OX2 9RU, UK

Library of Congress Control Number: 2005932574
ISBN 0-7618-3328-5 (paperback : alk. ppr.)

Dedication

David dedicates this book to his wife Natalie and three wonderful children, James, William, and Grace.

Roger dedicates this book to his wife Chris and their three amazing sons, Tyler, Timmy, and Ryan.

CONTENTS

PREFACE

One of the areas of greatest concern among many parents and legislators in the United States in 2005 is the problem of youth violence, particularly adolescent gun violence. Events such as the school shootings at Columbine and now Red Lake, Minnesota and media accounts of drive-by shootings in large urban areas serve as brutal reminders of the damage that guns can do in the wrong hands. Parents have responded to these fears by turning to home schooling and private schools in ever-increasing numbers. Legislators have responded by creating safe school zones and ever-increasing punitive punishments. School administrators have responded by passing zero tolerance rules, installing metal detectors, and generally increasing security at schools, both small and large. Thus, adolescent gun violence is a problem that permeates all layers of society.

Nevertheless, most indicators show that this concern may be misplaced. Levels of youth violence are significantly lower in 2005 than in the late 1980s and through most of the 1990s. The vast majority of children are not afraid to go to school and report that their school and communities are safe environments. Part of this disjunction between the public concerns regarding adolescent gun violence and its actual prevalence is due to a misunderstanding of the problem. While many citizens feel that youths, particularly youths in large urban areas, regularly carry guns and use them in crime, this is simply not the case. In this study, we attempt to add to the understanding of adolescent firearm violence by asking over 800 youth most familiar with guns (those who are currently incarcerated for their criminal activity) about their experiences with firearms. Through this effort, we hope to shed light on the actual sources, causes, and consequences of adolescent firearm activity.

David C. May
Richmond, Kentucky
May 2005

ACKNOWLEDGEMENTS

The authors wish to thank the Indiana Department of Correction for their cooperation and assistance in the administration of the survey for this study. They provided access to all of the youths in their facilities and worked with our research team to structure the time we spent at the facilities to maximize the quality of the data we received. We also would like to thank the staff of AIM (Aftercare for Indiana through Mentoring) who provided assistance in the administration of the survey. In particular, we thank Lori Carr, Chan Chanthaphone, Kathy DeBrabant, Holly Entstrasser, Allison Fetter-Harrott, Kelly Funk, Danielle Holzinger, Heath Hurst, Travis Hurst, Whitney Meagher, Bonnie Nixon, Andy Rule, Troy Schmitt, Jared Sigler, Samantha Stragliati, and Brian Thacker. Finally, we wish to thank Charles Mathew, Timothy McClure, and Pat Rooney for their assistance with the data analysis for this study.

CHAPTER 1

Gun Violence Among Young People: What Do We Know?

A high school student went on a shooting rampage on an Indian reservation Monday, killing his grandparents at their home and then seven people at his school, grinning and waving as he fired, authorities and witnesses said. The suspect apparently killed himself after exchanging gunfire with police. It was the nation's worst school shooting since the Columbine massacre in 1999 that killed 13 people. (Associated Press, March 22, 2005).

A gunman with an AK-47 rifle opened fire in a high school gym Monday, killing a 15-year-old boy and wounding three teenage girls in a spray of more than 30 bullets that sent students scrambling for cover. Four suspects, ranging in age from 15 to 19, were arrested in a sweep of the neighborhood near John McDonogh High School. Police Chief Eddie Compass said he did not know if the suspects attended the school. (Associated Press, April 14, 2003).

More young people have been killed or wounded by gunfire in the District this year, even though the city is seeing a decrease in crime including its overall homicide rate. So far, 17 youths under the age of 18 have been killed this year compared with a total of 12 last year. Almost 15 percent of the District's homicide victims this year have been children, and most of them were fatally shot. And, the rash of juvenile crime continues. Metropolitan Police said two 14-year-old girls and a 15-year-old boy were wounded in a drive-by shooting at about 11:30 p.m. Sunday in the 3900 block of Martin Luther King Avenue SE. Officer Kenneth Bryson, a spokesman for the Metropolitan Police Department, said the wounds were not considered to be life-threatening. The shooting might have stemmed from a fight with another group of teens at a party earlier in the evening. Crime involving the District's youth, such as Sunday's shooting, threatens to overshadow this year's decrease in crime throughout the city. As of yesterday, there have been 119 killings, compared with 163 at this time last year—a 27 percent decrease. The city is on pace to close the year with 190 homicides, a total that would be the lowest since 1985, when there were 147 slayings. Overall, assaults with a deadly weapon have fallen to 2,134 as of last

month, compared with 2,349 during the same period last year, according to pre-
liminary crime statistics. (Cella, August 17, 2004: B01).

These three stories are tragic testimonials to the impact of gun violence on
young people in the United States. In fact, there are three common themes
among the three stories: (1) the offenders and victims were all teenagers; (2) the
offenders, where identified, were all males; and (3) the offenders all used guns.
Victims were both male and female, the shootings occurred both on school
grounds and away from school grounds, two were in large urban areas while one
was in a rural area, and one incident used a semi-automatic assault rifle while
the others did not.

When United States residents think about youth gun violence in 2005, they
often think of Columbine and now, to a lesser extent, Red Lake Minnesota. The
school shootings that occurred in those settings serve as a tragic reminder of the
grim toll that guns have taken on youth. Nevertheless, far more common are
stories such as the third one, where youth engage in an argument, a fight erupts,
and gunplay occurs. These stories typify those that are often found in media
accounts of the nature and extent of gun violence among young people in the
United States. Nevertheless, these stories happen far less than the average citizen believes. Despite the rhetoric, gun possession and use by young people is a
relatively rare occurrence. The vast majority of young people never carry a gun
and even fewer ever use one in crime.

Despite its rarity, gun violence among young people is a problem that often
has tragic outcomes and thus is one that needs to be understood and cannot be
ignored. The point of this book is not to offer a universal solution to the problem
of gun violence among youth (although we do provide some recommendations
along that line). The point of this book is to give voices to those adolescent
males and females who are most familiar with guns and the motives of young
people behind the use of those guns. As such, in this book, we ask those youths
who have used guns in crime why they did so, where they obtained those guns,
and why they chose to use the guns that they did. Additionally, we attempt to
determine whether the guns that were used by the youths in this sample were
used primarily for protection, or if their usage brought about further violent activity. Based on these voices, we conclude by providing recommendations for
future research and policy.

The reader will not leave this book with a panacea for solving the problem
of gun violence among youth. More likely, the reader will leave this book with a
better understanding of the problem of gun violence among youth but will also
leave with further questions that need to be answered and further thoughts that
need to be developed. If that is the case, then we have accomplished the goal
that we set for ourselves prior to beginning this effort.

Adolescents, Firearms, and Crime: A Literature Review

Firearms play an important role in violent crime in the United States, both among adults and adolescents. In 2002, in almost three of four (71.1%) murder incidents where the weapon was known, the weapon used was a firearm. Within the firearm category, more than three in four firearms (76.6%) used in these murder incidents were handguns. Additionally, in over two in five (42.1%) robberies and one in ten violent crimes, the perpetrator used a firearm (Federal Bureau of Investigation 2003). Two-thirds (66.7%) of all murder victims and the vast majority (80.7%) of murder victims between the ages of thirteen and nineteen were killed by firearms (Federal Bureau of Investigation 2003).

Despite the fact that firearm death rates have been falling since the early 1990s for all age groups, beginning in 1986 and continuing until today, homicide (most of which has involved firearms) has evolved into the second-leading cause of death among youths aged fifteen to nineteen (Anderson 2002; Fingerhut and Christoffel 2002) and the fourth leading cause of death among all age groups below fifteen years of age (MacDorman et al. 2002). Among two groups, children under age twelve and youth between the ages of seventeen and nineteen, homicides account for 60 70% of all firearms deaths; for those between the ages of twelve and fifteen, homicides account for about 40% of all firearm deaths (Fingerhut and Christoffel 2002).

Snyder (2001) argues that the overall trend in murders among juveniles over the last two decades is all firearm-related. He demonstrates that while the juvenile firearm murder rate increased dramatically from 1981 to 1994, the juvenile nonfirearm murder rate remained stable throughout that same time period. Thus, it is apparent that firearms play a significant role in homicides and fatalities, particularly among young people in the United States.

The trends reflected in the aforementioned statistics, coupled with the public perception that youth crime was rising at much greater rates than was actually the case, led to a number of policies directed at reducing gun availability among youth. The 1994 Gun-Free Schools Act required that states receiving federal educational funds expel any student that brought a firearm to school. Additionally, nearly all states created enhanced criminal penalties for adults who assisted youth in obtaining firearms and one in three states banned minors from possessing any firearm (Butts et al. 2002). Butts and his associates (2002) suggest that policy changes made in reaction to firearm crimes among juveniles in the 1990s permanently changed the focus of the juvenile justice system from one that focused on rehabilitation to one that is "less individualized, more automatic, less confidential, and increasingly punitive" (Butts et al. 2002, 7). Thus, firearm possession and use among juveniles have significantly impacted the entire realm of juvenile justice. On any given day, some proportion of youths carry firearms, both at school and away from school. This section provides a review of the research on this subject.

Methodological Issues in Measuring Firearm Possession among Youth

There are methodological shortcomings that preclude researchers and policy makers from achieving consensus regarding the dynamics of adolescent gun use. There are three primary concerns: (a) the nature of the sample from which data are collected; (b) the length of time under study when respondents are asked about their firearms behaviors; and (c) the wording of the question(s) used to determine firearm possession. Each of these shortcomings is discussed in detail below.

Nature of Sample under Study

Researchers exploring the topic of possession and use of firearms among adolescents have used four different sources of data: a) arrest statistics; b) data about offenders whose guns were traced after they were used in crime; c) self-report data from samples of public high school students; and d) self-report data from samples of incarcerated youth. Each of these data sources presents unique challenges.

For instance, arrest statistics, by their nature, capture data only about youths who are actually arrested. Additionally, arrest data capture information about all youths arrested for *illegal possession of a deadly weapon*, not illegal possession of a firearm. As such, there are a small number of offenders arrested each year who illegally possess a deadly weapon that is not a firearm. While gun crime trace reports do capture data exclusively from offenders who use firearms, these data are also limited by the fact that they begin with arrest data. As such, neither presents a truly accurate picture of the incidence of youth arrested for firearm-related crimes nor incidence of firearm possession among youths throughout the United States.

Using data collected from samples of public high school students to examine firearm possession and use also presents a number of concerns. First and foremost, as with other forms of delinquent behavior, the vast majority of public high school students never carry or use firearms (see discussion below regarding the proportion of students carrying and using firearms). Secondly, while national studies do exist that examine firearm possession at school and in the community (e.g., National Longitudinal Youth Survey (NLYS), Youth Risk Behavior Surveillance (YRBS)), no such studies exist that regularly examine antecedents of firearm possession and use among adolescents. Thus, most of the studies that exist that provide detailed examination of the prevalence and predictors of firearm possession and behaviors use small, regional samples of adolescents. As such, the nature of the sample from one study to the next often creates vastly different estimates of the prevalence of firearm possession and use among public school students. The following review (while not exhaustive) presents numerous studies, detailing the type of sample used and the resulting estimates of prevalence of firearm possession based on those samples.

Official Data. One source of data regarding the incidence of illegal firearm possession among youth is arrest statistics. Annually, the Federal Bureau of Investigation (FBI) collects data from police departments throughout the United States and publishes the report, *Crime in the United States*, more commonly referred to as the Uniform Crime Reports (UCR). As mentioned earlier, these data, some of which were cited earlier, do not represent an entirely accurate portrayal of the incidence of firearm possession among young people. Nevertheless, the data for 2002 indicate that, of the 98,120 individuals arrested for illegal possession of a deadly weapon, 21,031 (21.4%) were under the age of 18 (Federal Bureau of Investigation 2003). While this statistic reveals little about the incidence of firearm possession among youth throughout the United States, it does indicate that youth represent a substantial portion of those who carry firearms and other deadly weapons illegally.

Another source of official data regarding the incidence of illegal firearm possession among youth is the *Crime Gun Trace Reports (2000)*, published by the Bureau of Alcohol, Tobacco, and Firearms (2002). Of the 88,570 trace requests processed by the BATF in 2000, slightly over three in five (54,241) of those requests included the age of the individual who possessed the gun for which the gun trace was initiated. Of that total, approximately one in thirteen (7.6%) firearms that were traced was possessed by an individual under the age of eighteen at the time the trace was conducted (U.S. Department of the Treasury 2002).

Thus, data from law enforcement agencies suggest that while youth comprise a small percentage of offenders arrested for both illegal possession of a deadly weapon and violent crimes committed with firearms in general, and gun trace data indicate that most of those individuals using guns in crime are adults, not youth, the fact still exists that a number of youth are engaged in illegal firearm behavior. As such, many researchers have turned to self-report data to examine both the prevalence and incidence of firearm possession among youth.

Surveys of Youths. As mentioned previously, there are at least two studies that provide national estimates of firearm possession among public school students. Grunbaum et al. (2002) and Kaufmann et al. (2001), analyzing data collected from 13,601 public school students as part of the Youth Risk Behavior Surveillance (YRBS) by the Centers for Disease Control, determined that one in twenty (5.5%) youth and one in ten males (10.3%) nationwide had carried a gun in the last thirty days. This proportion was slightly smaller than the previous year and thus maintained the decreasing trend in prevalence of firearm carrying in the last thirty days uncovered by the YRBS that began in 1993 (Kingery, Coggeshall, and Alford 1999). On the other hand, Luster and Oh (2001) examined data from 4,619 adolescent males collected as part of the National Longitudinal Survey of Youth in 1997. They determined that nine percent of the sample had carried a handgun in the past year and another seven percent had carried a handgun at an earlier time but not in the past year. Thus, using national data, somewhere between five and nine percent of public school students carry a gun each year; five percent have carried a gun in the last thirty days.

While a limited number of studies use data from national samples such as those outlined above, the vast majority of studies using data from public school students use local or regional samples. The advantage of utilizing this type of sample centers around the fact that there are extant studies of this genre that collect longitudinal data regarding firearm behaviors, thus allowing causal inferences in some cases where cross-sectional data only allow for association. One of the best of these data collection efforts is the Rochester Youth Development Study (RYDS). A number of researchers have used these data to make estimates regarding the extent of firearm possession among adolescents. Lizotte et al. (2000) and Lizotte and Sheppard (2001) examined data collected from 617 young men, originally interviewed as eighth graders and followed through ten subsequent waves. They found that (with the exception of waves eight, nine, and ten, where hidden gun carrying increased to 10%), five to six percent of the males surveyed had carried a hidden gun in the past six months. Bjerregaard and Lizotte (1995) used data from 987 students in waves seven through nine to distinguish between protective firearm ownership and firearm ownership for sport. Approximately nine percent of the sample owned guns for protection. Lizotte and Sheppard (2001) and Lizotte et al. (1996) examined data collected from males as part of wave four of the RYDS and determined that 4.4% of the sample owned guns for sport while 6.5% of the sample owned firearms for protection.

Arria, Wood, and Anthony (1995) also used longitudinal data collected from 1515 adolescents in an urban mid-Atlantic public school. Respondents were approximately nine years old at initial assessment and thirteen years old at time of responses used for the present study. They determined that one in ten boys (9.9%) and a small number of girls (1.4%) had carried a gun in the previous year.

Other studies have used cross-sectional data collected from small, regional samples of public school students to examine this issue. For instance, Callahan and Rivara (1992) used data collected from a sample of 970 eleventh graders in public schools in Seattle, Washington to determine that 6.4% of the students owned handguns. Hawkins et al. (2002), using a sample of 1465 students from a largely affluent community in a suburb of San Francisco (median household income was $68,790), determined that less than three (2.9) percent of the respondents had carried a gun for protection or in case of a fight. Hemenway et al. (1996) used data from a sample 752 seventh-graders and 440 tenth-graders collected in the spring of 1995 at twelve inner-city public schools in two large cities in the Northeast and Midwest. They determined that 17% of the sample had carried a concealed gun at some time in their life.

Sheley and Wright (1998) used a mail survey of sophomores and juniors from fifty-three high school sites throughout the United States to examine a number of factors associated with firearm possession among high school males.

Their strategy was laden with challenges that potentially biased their results. For instance, 60% of the high schools in their sampling frame declined to participate. Among the schools that did participate, only 45% of the students selected actually returned a completed questionnaire. The authors themselves suggest a potential "good boy" bias (Sheley and Wright 1998, 2). Nevertheless, even with the problematic nature of their data, 6% of the sample carried a gun outside the home "now and then" or "most of the time" during the past twelve months.

Sheley and Brewer (1995) used data from a sample of 418 tenth and eleventh graders from suburban public high schools in Louisiana. Almost one in five (18%) of the youth presently owned a handgun and 17% had carried a firearm, although the authors do not present the time period for which that question covered. Simon et al. (1998) used data from 2200 twelfth graders from high schools in six districts in California. They determined that 12.5% of the students had "carried a gun on yourself or in your car" in their lifetime.

Studies which focus more specifically on minority youths find higher rates of gun possession and gun carrying. Cunningham et al. (2000) examined data from 6,263 predominantly African-American students in elementary and middle schools in a nonmetropolitan area in a Southeastern state collected in the spring of 1996. They determined that almost half (46%) of the sample owned firearms, with nearly 30% of students owning pellet or BB guns, 14.4% owning rifles, nine percent owning pistols or handguns, and 4.4% owning some other type of gun. Over one in four (26.8%) students had carried a firearm outside their home in the past three months.

Webster, Gainer, and Champion (1993) examined data collected from 294 black adolescents in two public schools in Washington D.C. in 1991. They determined that 15.6% of the respondents had carried a gun with them for protection in their lifetime. Smith and Sheley (1995) used data from 825 female students in public schools in ten inner city high schools in five cities collected in the spring of 1991. They determined that nine percent of the females they interviewed had owned a revolver in their lifetime, while five percent of the students had owned an automatic or semiautomatic handgun. Seven percent owned a shotgun, while three percent indicated they had owned a hunting rifle, a sawed-off shotgun, and a military style rifle.

Smith (1996), Sheley (1994b), Sheley and Wright (1993a, 1993b), and Wright, Sheley, and Smith (1992) used data from 765 male students from inner city public schools from throughout the United States and found that one in five (22%) "owned or possessed" a firearm at the time the data were collected. One in seven students (15%) reported that they owned or possessed more than three firearms. Additionally, approximately one in eight (12%) carried a gun either "most" or "all" of the time.

Other studies have considered specifically whether students carried guns to school. Using data from 103 students from public schools in Louisiana, McNabb et al. (1996) determined that 20% of the group had carried a gun illegally at some point in their life. Summarizing data collected in 1996 from 6,169 students in grades six through twelve from twenty-one schools in Kentucky, Wilcox and Clayton (2001) determined that two percent of the students said they had taken a gun to school in the previous thirty days. Wilcox Rountree (2000) examined data collected from 4008 public high school students in grades six through twelve in three counties in Kentucky in 1996. She determined that 1.4% (Urban county), 1.7% (Western county), and approximately 3% (Eastern county) of the students responded that they had brought a firearm to school in the last thirty days (Wilcox Rountree 2000).

Orpinas, Murray, and Kelder (1999) found that, among their sample of 8,865 sixth, seventh, and eight graders in Texas, one in ten students had carried a handgun and slightly more had carried a weapon other than a handgun in the past thirty days. Simon et al. (1998) determined that, among their sample of 2200 high school seniors in California, one in five (21.8%) boys and one in twenty (5.3%) girls reported carrying a gun in their lifetime.

The preceding literature review reveals less consensus among researchers using regional samples of public school students than among researchers using the national samples reviewed above. Based on the research using these regional samples, the best estimate of thirty-day prevalence of gun carrying ranges between two and five percent of all youth (excluding inner city youth, where the rates may be slightly higher) while the best estimate of lifetime gun carrying is between 10 and 20%.

Surveys of Incarcerated Youths. A limited number of researchers have collected data from incarcerated adolescents regarding this phenomenon. These studies typically find much higher rates of gun ownership, possession, and use than those studies using samples of public school students. For example, Callahan, Rivara, and Farrow (1993) collected data from a convenience sample of 89 adolescent males detained in King County, Washington. They found that three in five (59.5%) of the subjects owned handguns. Seventy percent of the handgun owners reported carrying a gun to school within the last three years. Ash et al. (1996) used data collected from 63 juvenile offenders in Atlanta in 1995 to determine that most (84.1%) of the respondents had owned a gun at some point in their life while over three in four (77.8%) carried a gun at least occasionally and over one in three (38.1%) were "constant carriers," reporting that they carried a gun most or all of the time, prior to their incarceration. Webster et al. (2002) examined data from 45 males incarcerated in a juvenile justice facility in Maryland collected in 1998. Two in three (66.7%) had acquired at least one firearm in their lifetime.

Limber and Pagliocca (2000) determined that three in four (74.3%) incarcerated adolescent males had carried a handgun at some time in their life, and almost half (43.6%) had carried a rifle or shotgun. May (2001) determined that three in five (59.0%) respondents in a sample of 318 incarcerated adolescent males in Indiana had carried a gun for protection at some point in their life. Birkbeck and his associates (1999) used data collected from 380 confined juvenile offenders in New Mexico and determined that 82% of their sample had "owned or kept" a gun prior to their confinement (31).

In the most definitive series of studies to date, Sheley, Wright, and Smith published a number of studies based on data collected from a sample of 835 adolescent males incarcerated in juvenile facilities in various parts of the United States. Smith (1996), Sheley (1994a), Sheley and Wright (1993a, 1993b), and Wright et al. (1992) determined that four in five (83%) incarcerated juveniles either "owned or possessed" a gun just prior to their incarceration; two in three of the incarcerated juveniles (65%) owned or possessed three or more firearms at the time of their incarceration. Additionally, over half of the sample (55%) carried a gun either "most" or "all" of the time.

Wilkinson (2003) utilized data from 125 Black and Hispanic males from criminogenic neighborhoods in New York city. While the youth were in the community when interviewed, nine in ten (89.7%) had been incarcerated at some point in their life and thus closely resemble the incarcerated males reviewed in the studies above. As expected, these youth were heavily involved in firearm possession and use, as 91.8% of the respondents had possessed a gun at some point in their life and an even higher percentage (93.8%) had fired a gun. Respondents owned an average of 3.8 guns; four in five respondents carried a gun daily (29%) or on an occasional basis (52%).

Thus, as expected, the research using incarcerated samples of adolescents reveals much higher rates of firearm carrying. The best estimates for lifetime carrying of firearms among incarcerated adolescents range between 70 and 80% while the best estimates for 30-day firearm carrying range between 35 and 50%. Thus, it is safe to say that three in four incarcerated adolescent males have carried a gun in their lifetime and somewhere between one in two and one in three incarcerated adolescent males carried a firearm in the thirty days prior to their incarceration.

Length of Time under Study

Another methodological issue that has an impact on estimates of the prevalence of gun carrying among adolescents has to do with the window of time for which youths are asked to report about their gun ownership and carrying behaviors. Typically, researchers asks the respondents in their sample if/how many times they have carried a gun in the last 30 days (Grunbaum et al. 2002; Kingery et al. 1999; Lizotte et al. 2000, for example), if/how many times they have carried a gun in the past 12 months (Arria et al. 1995; Luster and Oh 2001, for example), or if they have *ever* carried or owned a gun (Birkbeck et al. 1999; Hemenway et al. 1996; May 2001; Webster et al. 1993, for example). As expected, these semantic differences often yield very different estimates of adolescent gun possession. As such, it is difficult to make meaningful comparisons between those youth who have carried a firearm in the last month and those youth who have carried a gun in their lifetime. This discrepancy contributes to the confusion regarding the prevalence of firearms as well.

Wording of Question

The final methodological concern in the research on adolescent firearm possession and use concerns the wording of the question used to ascertain firearm possession among adolescents. Numerous studies (most not reviewed here- see May (2001) for review) examine "weapon possession" both at school and away from school. Unfortunately, many of these studies do not distinguish between "weapons" in general and "firearms" specifically.

A number of studies use questions to assess only "weapon possession" and do not distinguish between types of weapons (Bailey, Flewelling, and Rosenbaum 1997; Kulig et al. 1998; Malek, Chang, and Davis 1998). Other researchers list several weapons in the question assessing weapon possession (DuRant et al. 1995). Still others (Hawkins et al. 2002) assess weapons possession in general, then specify what type of weapon was carried (e.g., what percentage of weapon carriers carried a firearm), but only report predictors of weapon possession in general in their multivariate models. Some researchers (see Rountree 2000; Wilcox and Clayton 2001, for example) do not uncover enough firearm carrying among their sample to use multivariate statistical techniques while others (Simon, Crosby, and Dahlberg 1999) combine firearm possession with other types of weapon possession and include the two together as a summated dependent variable. Finally, others (Malecki and Demaray 2003, for example) ask the respondent only if they have taken a gun or another weapon to school and make no attempt to measure gun carrying or possession outside of the school setting.

Even among those studies that concentrate on firearms prevalence outside of the school setting either exclusively or combined with firearm prevalence in schools, there are a wide variety of questions used to ascertain firearm possession and use. The most common means of assessing firearm prevalence among adolescents appears to be asking youth whether and/or how often they carry firearms, either as a stand-alone measure or as an option when asking about weapon possession in general (Grunbaum et al. 2002; Hemenway et al. 1996; Orpinas et al. 1999; McNabb et al. 1996). This question is a good measure of gun possession but a weaker measure of gun ownership, as adolescents may carry guns owned by someone else (see Sheley and Wright 1993, for discussion).

An alternative strategy for measuring gun prevalence among adolescents involves asking the respondent whether he or she *owns* a firearm (Birkbeck et al. 1999; Callahan and Rivara 1992; Callahan et al. 1993). Other researchers ask about ownership then distinguish between purposes of firearm ownership—such as protection, sport, or collection (Cunningham et al. 2000; Lizotte et al. 1994; Bjerregaard and Lizotte 1995). These are good measures of firearm ownership but weaker measures of gun possession, as youth may own firearms but never carry them outside the home, or carry them only on special outings (e.g., hunting, target shooting).

Yet another rubric for assessing firearm prevalence specifically asks about carrying a firearm for protection (Hawkins et al. 2002; May 2001, for example) but does not ask about carrying for sport or ownership. The intent of these researchers is often to understand the nature of firearm possession for protection (the most commonly cited reason for possession among adolescents) and, as such, is a weak measure of general firearm ownership and excludes all adolescents who carry firearms for reasons other than protection (although research by Sheley and Wright 1993 and May 2001 indicates that may be a small percentage of firearm carriers in any sample).

Finally, the most infrequent (and perhaps the best) measure to assess the prevalence of firearm carrying and use among adolescents involves the qualitative measurement of this phenomenon. Some researchers use open-ended instruments assessing a number of issues regarding violence and victimization, and characterize gun owners as those who mention having owned or carried a gun in the interview (Ash et al. 1996; Wilkinson 2003). As such, these studies allow the youth to self-report their firearm activity in a larger context of other behaviors and activities. Consequently, the interviewee is not limited to the responses provided by the researcher and may offer specific insight into the nature and characteristics of ownership and use of firearms that self-report surveys in other formats may not allow. This type of operationalization is uncommon in this area of research.

Regardless of the type of youth used (whether incarcerated youth or samples in public schools), administrators of the facilities (typically, public schools or juvenile detention facilities) where the youth are located are reluctant to allow researchers the time to conduct the type of qualitative research necessary to use the strategy used above. As such, the vast majority of research in this area continues to be self-report, quantitative research. Due to the methodological issues described above, it is difficult to make specific generalizations regarding either prevalence or incidence of firearm possession and ownership. Further, it is also difficult to develop consistent generalizations regarding demographic and contextual predictors of firearm possession and use as well. In this review, we turn next to the demographic and contextual variables that have demonstrated an association with firearm possession among adolescents.

Demographic Factors Related to Firearm Possession Among Youths

A number of studies have examined firearm and other weapon possession among adolescents (Arria, Wood, and Anthony 1995; Ash et al. 1996; Asmussen 1992; Birkbeck et al. 1999; Blumstein 1995; Callahan and Rivara 1992; Callahan, Rivara, and Farrow 1993; Chandler et al. 1998; Durant et al. 1995, 1997; Harris 1993; Kann et al. 2000; Kulig et al. 1998; Lizotte et al. 1994; May 1999; McNabb et al. 1996; Roth 1994; Sheley and Brewer 1995; Sheley and Wright 1993; Sheley 1994; Smith and Sheley 1995; U.S. Department of Justice 2000a; U.S. Department of Justice 2000b; Webster, Gainer and Champion 1993; Wilson and Zirkel 1994). The vast majority of these researchers agree that: (1) males, (2) gang members, (3) those youth whose peers carry weapons and engage in other forms of delinquency, and (4) those who are more likely to engage in other deviant behaviors are more likely to carry weapons (both firearms and weapons other than firearms). Additionally, the vast majority of these studies indicate that protection is the primary reason youth carry weapons to school. There is less agreement regarding the impact of socioeconomic status, age, victimization experience, and ethnicity on adolescent firearm possession and use. Each of these predictors is considered separately here.

Gender

The most consistent finding in the area of firearm possession and use among adolescents is that males are more likely to carry and use firearms than females, as practically every researcher that has examined the impact of gender on firearm possession and use has uncovered this relationship (e.g., Callahan and Rivara 1992; Cunningham et al. 2000; Hemenway et al. 1996; Sheley and Brewer 1995; Simon et al. 1998). This finding is intuitive for a number of reasons. First, it is well documented that males are significantly more likely to engage in delinquency of practically all types (Wilson and Herrnstein 1985). Additionally, among adults, males are far more likely to own firearms than females (Wright, Rossi, and Daly 1983). The combination of these findings would suggest that males of all ages are more likely to own and carry firearms; defining that act as illegal for juveniles does not appear to alter that finding.

Age

The evidence on the relationship between age and gun possession and use is less consistent. While young adults are far more likely to commit both firearm and non-firearm crimes (Federal Bureau of Investigation 2003), when the research focuses exclusively on adolescents, the relationship is not as clear. Grunbaum et al. (2002) determined that age had an inverse association with firearm possession, as ninth graders were more likely than twelfth graders to admit carrying a firearm. On the other hand, Callahan et al. (1993) found no significant age differences in handgun ownership among the incarcerated males they surveyed. Sheley and Brewer (1995) also found no statistically significant association between age and either handgun ownership or carrying. As such, the evidence is contradictory regarding the impact of age on firearm possession and use.

Delinquent Peers and Peers Who Own Guns for Protection

Luster and Oh (2001) determined that those youth under the age of fifteen in their sample who had friends, siblings, or cousins in a gang were more likely to carry firearms while those youth over the age of fifteen who had peers who engaged in problem behavior were more likely to carry firearms. Lizotte et al. (1994) determined that those youth whose peers held delinquent values were significantly more likely to own guns for protection but not for sport than their counterparts. Additionally, Lizotte et al. (2000) determined that having peers who own guns for protection increased the likelihood that a youth would carry a hidden gun. Bjerregaard and Lizotte (1995), Lizotte et al. (1994), and Lizotte and Sheppard (2001) determined that those youth who own guns for protection were significantly more likely to have friends who also own guns for protection while Cunningham et al. (2000) determined that those youth whose peers engaged in "high-risk" gun ownership were significantly more likely to engage in high-risk gun ownership as well. These studies paint a consistent picture: adolescents whose peers own guns are significantly more likely to own, carry, and use firearms as well.

Gang Membership

Luster and Oh (2001) determined that those youth who were involved in gangs were more likely to carry firearms than their counterparts who were not involved in gangs. Lizotte et al. (2000) and Bjerregaard and Lizotte (1995) used longitudinal data to determine that gang members were significantly more likely to own and carry guns; however, the effect of gang membership on gun possession fades with age. By the seventh wave of data collection, the impact of gang membership on gun possession completely disappears. Lizotte and Sheppard (2001) found that gang members were more likely to own firearms for protection but not sport. Callahan and Rivara (1992) determined that gang members were over eight times more likely to own handguns than their counterparts who were not gang members. Callahan et al. (1993) determined that gang members in their sample of incarcerated males were more likely to own handguns while Sheley and Wright (1993a) determined that joining a gang made both inner city high school males and incarcerated males more likely to carry and own a gun. Gang membership appears to be a factor that influences the likelihood of carrying and using firearms.

Race

Although several studies indicate that nonwhites are more likely to carry firearms (Durant et al. 1997; Bjerregaard and Lizotte 1995; Lizotte et al. 2000) numerous studies either find no statistically significant racial differences in adolescent firearm possession or find that whites are more likely to carry firearms than nonwhites. For example, Luster and Oh (2001) used a national sample of adolescent males and determined that for those less than 15 years of age, whites were more likely to carry a firearm than blacks or Hispanics while among those over fifteen years of age, there were no statistically significant racial differences in firearm possession. Lizotte et al. (1994) determined that whites were significantly more likely to own guns for protection and for sport than their black counterparts. Callahan et al. (1993) found no statistically significant racial differences in handgun ownership among the incarcerated males they surveyed (see also Simon et al. 1998 and Sheley and Brewer 1995). As with age, then, there is no consistent evidence that race is associated with the possession and use of firearms by adolescents. Brown (2004) suggests this is one area that needs further exploration, as the impact of race on adolescent firearm possession also appears to be dependent on the sample under study and the operationalization of firearm possession and carrying.

Socioeconomic Status

Findings from the limited number of studies that examine the relationship between socioeconomic status and adolescent firearm possession are contradictory at best (Brown 2004). While some researchers suggest that youth from lower socioeconomic strata are more likely to possess firearms (Callahan and Rivara 1992; Callahan et al. 1993; Wilcox and Clayton 2001) others (Kulig et al. 1998; May 2001; May 1999) find no statistically significant relationship between the two. Further exploration is needed in this area.

Victimization Experience

A number of researchers have also determined that youth who had been previously victimized or threatened with victimization are more likely to carry weapons both to school (Simon et al. 1999; Wilcox and Clayton 2001) and away from school (Simon et al. 1999; Webster et al. 1993) although others find no relationship between victimization (either threatened or actual) and weapon possession (May 2001; Wilcox Rountree 2000). As such, this relationship is far from conclusive. It does appear, however, that youths who have been victimized are more likely to carry guns for protection.

Involvement in Other Delinquent Activity

One of the most consistent predictors of adolescent firearm possession and use is an adolescent's involvement with delinquency, crime, and other deviant behaviors. In practically every study reviewed here, those youths who were most likely to carry firearms were also significantly more likely to engage in delinquent or criminal activity (Bjerregaard and Lizotte 1995; Callahan and Rivara 1992; Callahan et al. 1993; May 2001; Sheley and Brewer 1995; Webster et al. 1993; Wilcox Rountree 2000; Wilcox and Clayton 2001). Blumstein (1995) suggests that much of the increase in youth violence that continued into the early 1990s was primarily due to adolescent drug distribution. Kulig et al. (1998), on the other hand, argue that adolescent firearm possession is just another deviant activity in a deviant adolescent's web of delinquent activities. As such, regardless of the sample under study or the operationalization of firearm possession, youth who engage in the most delinquent activity are more likely to possess firearms as well.

What We Know about the Involvement of Adolescents with Firearms

As a recap to this literature review, we note the following conclusions. Most researchers agree that the vast majority of nonincarcerated adolescents do not carry firearms. Additionally, the proportion of incarcerated youth who have carried firearms (either explicitly for protection or not) is much greater than the proportion of nonincarcerated youths who have carried firearms. Among both groups, males, gang members, those youths who engage in delinquent and criminal activities, those youths from criminogenic neighborhoods, and those youths who perceive themselves most at risk are significantly more likely to carry firearms than their counterparts. On the other hand, and despite popular conjecture and media portrayals of "older, gun-carrying, poor, black youth," the relationship between firearm possession and age, race, and socioeconomic status is far from conclusive—even those researchers that do find a relationship between these factors call for additional research to disentangle those relationships. Finally, youths who have been victimized may or may not be more likely to carry firearms.

The Current Study

In this study, we seek to add to the extant literature in two ways. First, we replicate the research by Sheley and Wright (1995). We view their work as the seminal work in the area of adolescent gun possession. Sheley and Wright (1995) used a sample of incarcerated youth to determine: (a) the sources from which adolescent gun carriers obtain their firearms; (b) the types of guns that adolescent gun carriers prefer; and (c) the reasons behind why adolescents choose the guns they prefer to carry. The data on which their research was built were collected in early 1991, at the peak of the youth "violent crime wave" discussed earlier. As such, we feel it is important to replicate that work a decade later to determine if the patterns that emerged in their data still hold true today.

We also extend the research of May (2001a, 2001b) by testing the fear of criminal victimization hypothesis while controlling for theoretical predictors of adolescent firearm possession. May (2001a) suggests that adolescents make defensive adaptations to fear due to the limited opportunity to avoid fear by constrained behaviors. One of the defensive adaptation strategies he proposes is weapon possession for protection. Most previous work in this area did not consider whether fear of victimization led to carrying a weapon for protection. Adolescents were simply asked why they carry a weapon (sport, protection, status, and so on). May (2001a) and Webster et al. (1993) suggest that the factors that drive firearm possession for protection are somewhat different than those factors that drive possession of weapons other than firearms (e.g., knives, blunt instruments) for protection. Thus, we consider it imperative to examine predictors of defensive *gun* possession.

Adolescents make defensive adaptations to fear of crime. Thus, fear of crime may lead to defensive gun possession among certain adolescents. Intuitively, then, those most fearful of criminal victimization might also be those most likely to carry weapons for protection and to join gangs for protection. Although many researchers have emphasized the relationship between weapons, gangs, and delinquency (see Blumstein 1995, for example), only May (2001a) has examined it from the perspective of the fear of criminal victimization hypothesis. In his study, May examined the role of fear in contributing to such defensive behaviors as weapon possession for protection and gang membership for protection, and to subsequent violent activity. Results of the May study found that fear of victimization did not lead to defensive weapon possession or gang membership.

In this study, we focus on the factors associated with protective gun possession and the impact on violent delinquency that may result from these defensive adaptations. We improve upon the work of May (2001a) by adding theoretical predictors in an attempt to explain violent delinquency. We suggest that fear of criminal victimization will indirectly affect engagement in violent activity through weapon possession for protection and gang membership for protection. We also extend May's work by considering the way that fear is measured in a sample of adolescents. We believe that adolescents that have already engaged in delinquency and are serving time in a correctional facility are unlikely to report being afraid of being victimized. Yet, we do not believe this means that they are not afraid. In fact, despite reporting that they are not afraid of being victimized, they are reporting carrying guns and other weapons and joining gangs for the purpose of protection. They are also reporting a high likelihood of potential victimization. Thus, we argue that perceived risk of victimization may be a more valid way of tapping fear of victimization in this population. As such, we examine the fear of criminal victimization hypothesis with perceived risk of victimization as a proxy for fear of criminal victimization and determine whether this association continues after controlling for well-established theoretical predictors of delinquency.

The rest of the book is organized as follows. In chapter 2, we discuss the methods through which we collected the data used for this study and the operationalization of the variables under study here. Each of the five chapters that follow begins with a brief literature review of the topic at hand then concludes with the results from the data that we collected for this study. In chapter 3, we examine the sources of gun acquisition for the youth. We follow that with an examination of which guns juveniles prefer in chapter 4 and the reasons for those preferences in chapter 5. In chapter 6, we seek to determine whether the youth under study here engage in "protective" or "aggressive" gun possession. We then examine the impact of protective gun possession on violent activity (controlling for well-known theoretical explanations of delinquency) in chapter 7. We conclude the book by reviewing the findings and suggesting policy implications based on those results in chapter 8. Our goal is that upon completion of this book, the reader will have developed a better understanding of adolescent firearm possession, its causes, and its consequences.

CHAPTER 2

Methodology

Data

The data used in this study were collected during the months of January and February 2002 at nine state-run correctional facilities in Indiana. Permission was received from the Indiana Department of Correction to administer a self-report survey to all juveniles housed at these facilities. All of the youths in the facilities at that time of the survey were eligible to participate. Participation was optional for the individual youths. The questionnaire was administered to the youths in groups of between fifteen and seventy-five, depending on the facility. Typically, the youths were seated at tables of four or more youths, although in one facility, the youths were seated at individual desks. Residents were assured of their ano-nymity by the researchers; facility staff either stayed away from the room or remained in the room for supervision of larger groups but did not interact with the youths during the administration of the survey. This was done to ensure that the staff's effect on the honesty of the respondents would be negligible. Youths were allowed approximately one hour to complete the surveys. In most of the sites, the juvenile offenders were provided with a candy bar at the completion of the questionnaire.

The survey was administered on separate dates to each facility over the course of a two-month period. On the day of the administration of the survey, we sought to include every youth at the facility. Depending on the size of the group to participate and the number of different locations at each facility work-ing on the survey at the same time, one of the authors led a team of assistants in the administration. All of the assistants were trained in the administration of the survey. As much as possible, the survey was administered orally, in that one person in each room read the questions out loud while the youths completed their own questionnaire at their individual seat. This was done to minimize comprehension issues and to keep the youths engaged in the survey until it was complete. With the blessing of the Department of Correction, we were provided access to most of the youths in each facility. This included any youths who were temporarily housed on the segregation units. Despite this, on the day we were at each facility, there were a small number of youths who were unavailable to complete the survey because they were temporarily engaged in another activity and then could not be made available at an alternative time because of the structure of the facility schedule. In all but one of the facilities, the research team was able to present the option of participation in the survey to the youths themselves. This typically led to greater participation on the part of the youths.

In spite of all the procedures we put into place to maximize the quality of the date, not all of the youths provided usable data. Some youths elected not to complete the entire survey and depending on the sections they left blank, may not have provided the data for the analyses here. Others clearly did not take the survey seriously, as could be determined by patterns in their responses (i.e., responses were provided in a pattern that showed the question itself was not being answered, such as a sequence of 1, 2, 3, 4, 5, 6, or a series of 6s or 1s or some other number). When we could determine that the youth did not take the survey seriously, the data were removed from the sample early in the data cleaning stage. All in all, approximately 60% of the facility residents completed usable questionnaires for a final sample of 828 respondents.

These facilities represent the universe of settings within the state juvenile correctional system in Indiana. As such, there is a range of security levels represented here. In addition, the facilities ranged in capacity from 40 to 360. The participants were classified to the different facilities based on gender, calculated risk for reoffending, and additional considerations about the type of offending behavior exhibited, and special needs of the youths. For instance, Facility 8 housed the adolescent sex offender treatment program for the boys. It was also the facility for the boys with the best treatment available for those with mental health needs (including psychotropic medications). Facility 9 was the facility that specialized in substance abuse treatment and was the location boys were likely to be assigned to if the key criminogenic need was substance abuse. Beyond these distinctions, we present here a basic description of the types of youths housed at each facility.

- Facility 1: This facility provided a boot camp program for adolescent males. To be assigned to this facility, youths must meet some basic physical requirements. The youths housed at this facility were classified as low risk. The facility had a capacity of seventy youths.
- Facility 2: This facility held forty boys and was a minimum-to-medium security facility. The youths classified to this facility tended to be low or medium risk and from the northern part of the state, to facilitate visitation from the family.
- Facility 3: This was the largest facility for boys in the state, with a capacity of 360 beds. It was less than two years old and housed the highest risk boys—those classified as high risk or very high risk.
- Facility 4: This facility was the newest boys' facility in the state and had a capacity of 100. The boys at this facility were medium or high risk.

- Facility 5: This facility was the smallest facility in the state and housed about thirty girls at one time. The girls assigned to this facility were the lowest risk girls incarcerated in the state facilities.
- Facility 6: This facility was a fifty-bed minimum-security institution for boys. The lowest-risk boys in the state were assigned to this facility.
- Facility 7: This is the facility where the majority of girls were sent in this state. This facility had the widest variety of risk levels of any facility, with girls ranging from the highest risk to the lowest risk all on the same grounds, separated into groups (housed in different cottages) based on risk and age.
- Facility 8: This was the oldest male facility in the state, with a capacity of 335 beds. As described above, this facility provided very specific forms of treatment that were unique among the different facilities in the state system. The youths classified to this facility were the highest risk cases, similar to those classified to Facility 3.
- Facility 9: This facility was a medium-to-high risk facility that housed 160 youths, along with the parole violators unit. As described above, the key treatment program at this facility was substance abuse.

Sample Characteristics

The adolescents comprising this sample have, for the most part, engaged in serious or chronic forms of delinquency, resulting in commitment to the state correctional system from their local county juvenile court. The prevalence rates for the various types of delinquency used in this study are presented in table 2.1. It is clear that this sample is highly involved in criminal activity. The youths in this sample have also engaged in a number of different criminal activities. Over 70% of the sample had previously consumed alcoholic beverages. Similarly, over 70% of this sample reported having used marijuana previously. Over two-thirds of the sample admitted to having been guilty of disturbing the peace (loud, rowdy, or unruly in a public place). A similarly high percentage (67%) of the sample had knowingly bought, sold or held something that was stolen. Also, about that many subjects (67%) reported having committed an assault on a schoolmate or a teacher. Almost that many (65%) reported having assaulted someone other than a schoolmate, teacher, or family member.

Over 60% of the full sample reported having been drunk in a public place. Over 60% of the sample also had previously sold marijuana. Prevalence rates were over 50% for illegal gambling (57%), and joyriding (52%). When we consider the more serious forms of violent offending, we find relatively high rates of participation. Over 40% reported having taken part in a gang fight. An equally high percentage reported having used a weapon to commit a crime. This was also true of those reporting having committed an aggravated assault. If we combined the measures of robbery into one index, we find that 29% of the sample had taken part in a robbery previously. Similarly, our composite measure of violent offending (described in more detail below) shows that over 80% of the sample had engaged in some form of violent crime.

The youths in the sample were also more likely to engage in defensive behaviors, as over 40% reported having carried a gun for protection. As such, this sample is not representative of all adolescents. The sample selected for this analysis was also not representative of the population of youths in juvenile correctional facilities at large. As Sheley and Wright suggest, a sample of incarcerated youths can provide us with an important perspective

> both by virtue of their extreme behavior and the fact that they 'got caught'. . .
> the source of much gunplay and violence about which this study is interested.
> These youth likely are responsible for a very high percentage of the serious
> crime committed by juveniles, and are far more criminal than the most criminal
> of nonincarcerated youth (see Cernkovich, Giordano, and Pugh 1985). They
> were apprehended and incarcerated because they committed so many serious
> crimes that the odds finally caught up with them. (1995, 12)

The participants in this study included adolescent males and females from throughout the state. A number of descriptive statistics for the sample are presented in table 2.2. Only 18% of the juveniles reported living in a household with both their biological parents prior to their incarceration. The most common family structure was for the youths to live with their mother only (32% of the sample), with another 20% living with one biological parent and a stepparent. Only 21% of the youths in the sample reported that their biological parents were currently married to one another. The respondents reported an average of four siblings, and the bulk of the youths lived in a home with four or fewer siblings. While 26% of the sample reported having lived in their home for ten or more years, 12% reported having lived at the current address (prior to their incarceration, that is) for less than one year, and another 17% had lived at that address for between one and two years. Seventeen percent of the juveniles in this study reported having children.

We also asked the youths about their educational experiences. School involvement had (by and large) been problematic for these juveniles. Very few of the youths had even attended school in the eleventh or twelfth grade. Over half of the youths reported average grades in school of C or lower. While almost half (49%) of the youths said they would like to earn a college degree, only 31% believed it was possible. Almost all (94%) reported that they had been suspended from school at some point. In addition, nearly two-thirds (64%) had been expelled from school at least once and almost half (47%) had repeated at least one grade in school.

The youths reported information about the socioeconomic status of their families. These responses are presented in table 2.3. Only about half of the fathers and half of the mothers were reported to be working full time. Among the parents who were working, the mothers were most likely to work in a governmental job or a service job. Over 20% of the fathers were employed in construction. Less than 10% of the fathers worked in managerial or professional positions, whereas nearly 16% had such jobs. Just over 20% of the mothers had not even earned a high school diploma. Almost 30% of the fathers had never completed high school. Almost equal proportions of the mothers and fathers (nearly 30%) had completed some post-secondary education.

Survey Instrument

The questionnaire used to collect the data for this study consisted of a number of Likert-type questions randomly ordered using a six-point scale with "strongly agree" and "strongly disagree" at the extreme ends. These questions were used to examine attitudes and beliefs of the subjects, particularly as they related to problem solving skills, empathy towards their victims, locus of control, self esteem, risk taking, impressions about the police and the courts, anger control, perceptions of blocked opportunities, and social morality. A number of questions were also included to assess the quality of the youth's neighborhood. Several questions were included to capture information about the structure and socioeconomic status of the family, the school experiences of the youths, and the leisure time habits of the youths. Several indicators were also included to represent various theoretical explanations of crime. Finally, a number of questions were included that have frequently been used in other studies (see, for example, Elliott, Huizinga, and Ageton 1985; May 1999) to capture self-reports of victimization and delinquent activity.

Finally, as the focus of this study was a detailed examination of patterns and predictors of acquisition and use of firearms, a number of questions were also included to collect data on these experiences. The entire questionnaire used to collect the data for this study is included in the Appendix. The actual instrument was formatted so that it met the criteria for "attractive" self-report questionnaires (e.g., wide margins, not cluttered, flowed consistently, large font). To conserve space, we present only the questions, statements, responses, and bridge statements in the Appendix. Copies of the properly formatted questionnaire are available from the authors upon request.

Variables Used in Analyses

Throughout the remainder of this book, results from a number of analyses will be presented. In this section, we describe the operationalization of these variables and provide some data on the distribution of values for these variables. Data are provided here in three different tables. Data depicting the delinquent activities of the youths are presented in table 2.1 while descriptive information about the youths themselves, their family, and their school experiences is presented in table 2.2 and table 2.3. Data on the various scales and indexes that we created for the analyses in the later chapters are presented in tables 2.4 and 2.5.

Protective Gun Possession

A key variable for our analyses throughout this book is whether the youths had chosen to carry a firearm for their own personal protection. As will be shown in the next several chapters, the previous literature is clear that the primary reason that teenagers secure and carry guns is for protection. In this survey, the youths were asked to indicate whether they had "carried a gun for protection." This variable is a dichotomous measure coded 1 if they ever carried a gun for protection. In this sample, 41% reported having carried a gun for protection previously (see table 2.1).

Violent Activity

For the purposes of this study, we are most interested in whether access to guns contributes to the commission of violent offenses. To examine this relationship, we consider both a composite measure of violent delinquency, and we examine whether the impact of gun carrying is more important in the case of a violent crime where the use of a gun is most likely. For our study, we focus specifically on robbery.

From the number of different offenses for which we asked the youths to provide self-report data about, we selected five to incorporate into an index of violent offending. Respondents were asked to indicate if they had ever done the following: used a weapon to commit a crime, been involved in a gang fight, used force (strong-arm methods) to get money or things from people other than family members or schoolmates, hit or threatened to hit someone other than a schoolmate, teacher, or family member, and attacked someone with the idea of seriously hurting or killing him/her. In its final form, this composite measure is coded 1 if the youths have reported committing any of these offenses and 0 if they reported committing none of them. In this sample, 81% of the youths reported engaging in at least one of these violent offenses.

Our selection of the five behaviors to include in this index of violent offending was based on a number of factors. First and foremost, we identified the behaviors that we judged to be the most serious forms of violence that we examined in our survey. Second, we considered the ability of this measure to distinguish in a meaningful way between youths in our sample. With an additional two items included in the index, for instance, the prevalence rate was over 90%. Third, we used factor analysis to examine the internal consistency between the different measures we sought to include on this measure. Using this approach, we found that our measure of rape (had or tried to have sexual relations with someone against their will) did not fit very well in an index of violent crime. As such, it was not included in this index.

The vast majority of the respondents had engaged in one or more of the violent activities under study. As such, we were interested in determining whether gun carrying was important in predicting involvement in a particular type of violent offense where the use of a gun is likely to be a feature. For our purposes, we considered robbery. Two individual items from the survey have been combined to create an index of robbery. These items include using force (strong-arm methods) to get money or things from schoolmates and from people other than family members and schoolmates. This measure is also coded as a dichotomy, with 1 indicating that the youth has engaged in at least one of the behaviors, and 0 indicating that the youth has never engaged in robbery, as defined here. For this sample, we determined that 29% had engaged in robbery previously.

Demographic Characteristics

Throughout the analyses, we control for a number of demographic factors. As discussed in the previous chapter, these variables have demonstrated either strong or moderate relationships with protective gun possession. The distribution of these variables is provided in table 2.1. We discuss the operationalization of each of those variables here.

One of the variables we controlled for was gender. As reflected in table 2.1, four in five respondents in this sample were male. In each of the models included in the remaining chapters, males are coded (1) while females are coded (0) on this measure.

To control for race, we constructed a measure from the data from the surveys. Respondents were asked to respond to a question asking them how they "described" themselves. Response categories included: "African American/Black", "White", "American Indian", "Mexican American/Latino", "Asian or Asian American", and "Other." Within the sample, 49% of the respondents were Caucasian and 35% were African-American, with smaller percentages of respondents from each of the other categories. As the number of minority youths was quite small with the exception of African-Americans, we collapsed the nonwhites into one category and created a dummy variable in which nonwhites were coded 1 and whites were coded 0. Respondents who described themselves as anything other than white were included in the nonwhite category.

As May (2001) and others have argued, measurement of socioeconomic status among adolescents is a difficult task. As such, we chose to replicate the measure used by May (2001) to simply distinguish between those who are "poor" and those who were not. Respondents were asked to indicate whether their family had "...received some form of public assistance (such as WIC, AFDC/welfare, or food stamps)" in the past year. One in three (33%) youth reported that their families received some form of public financial assistance in the previous year.

Finally, we include age as a control variable in the analyses to follow. Respondents were also asked to indicate "how old" they were. Respondents ranged in age from 12 to 20, and the average age was 16.

Violent Victimization Experience

As the literature reviewed in the previous chapter suggests, the relationship between violent victimization experience and protective gun carrying is inconclusive. As such, we controlled for violent victimization experience as well.

Respondents were asked whether they "had someone threaten to hurt me" or "had someone threaten to hurt me at school." An index was created to indicate whether the youths had been victimized in either way. Youth who reported having been threatened were coded 1 on this new measure of personal victimization. If they indicated that neither had happened to them in the past, then they were coded as 0 on this measure. In this sample, 78% of the youths reported having been victimized previously.

Perception of Neighborhood Incivility

One of the best predictors of whether a youth carries a gun for protection is their perception of their neighborhood. Youths from criminogenic neighborhoods typically are more likely to carry weapons than their counterparts from less troubled neighborhoods (see May 2001 for review). As such, we created an index to represent perceptions of "neighborhood incivility." Using factor analysis we identified a number of items that fit together in one factor. Six items were selected to capture neighborhood incivilities: (1) I feel safe from crime in my neighborhood; (2) In my neighborhood, people will call the police right away if they think a crime is being committed; (3) My neighborhood is noisy and the streets always seem to have litter on them; (4) There are gangs in my neighborhood; (5) My neighborhood is getting worse all of the time; and (6) Most of the people living in my neighborhood are good, upstanding citizens. Since not all of the items were coded in a way that the high values corresponded to greater incivility, we reverse-coded the first two and the last item and then summed the scores across the six items. Statistics for this index are reported in table 2.5.

Perception of Risk of Victimization

As May (2001) and others have suggested, perception of risk of victimization is one of the most important determinants of protective gun possession. In this survey we asked the youths to rate the likelihood (on a scale of 1 to 10) that the following would happen to them in the coming year: have someone break into your house while your family is away; be raped or sexually assaulted; be murdered; be attacked by someone with a weapon; have something that belongs to you taken from you; and be robbed or mugged. Using factor analysis, we created a scale that incorporates the responses to these items into a single measure. Using the factor analysis procedure in SPSS, we created a factor score for each respondent that incorporated their responses to all of these items. Because of the varying levels of severity represented by the items in this scale, we chose not to create a summated index that treats the different items as being of equal weight. Instead we allowed the factor analysis results to weight the items based on the statistical associations among the items. Statistics for this scale are reported in table 2.5.

Theoretical Indices

In chapter seven, we examine the ability of a number of theoretical perspectives to predict both gun-related and violent delinquency. We consider four theoretical perspectives in particular: differential association, nonsocial reinforcement, strain, and social control. For each of these theories, we construct a composite measure that captures a key aspect of the explanation as to why youths engage in delinquency. From the survey data, we explored several composite measures using factor analysis. Based on our factor analyses (we used principal component analysis in all of the analyses reported in this chapter), we identified four measures that met the standards of internally consistent scales. Factor analysis results supported the conclusion that the items fit together in one factor, with factor scores of .500 or higher for each item within the factor and reliability analysis results (Cronbach's alpha) that demonstrated acceptable to good levels of internal consistency. Statistics for each scale are included in table 2.5.

For differential association, we were interested in capturing the influence of peers. We constructed a scale using six items from the survey. Youths were asked to indicate the extent to which they agreed or disagreed with the following statements: my best friends disapprove of people trying drinks of an alcoholic beverage; my best friends disapprove of people taking illegal drugs occasionally; my best friends disapprove of people smoking one or more packs of cigarettes per day; most of the people I associate with would never break the law; if I were thinking of breaking the law, my friends would tell me not to do it; and, my best friend encourages me to continue my education after high school. Higher values on this scale represent more disagreement with these items, thus representing more antisocial peers. As we see in table 2.5, the reliability for this scale was acceptable (alpha = .741).

For nonsocial reinforcement, we wanted to capture the inclination of the youths toward risk taking. The scale we assembled used seven items from the survey. Youths were asked to indicate the extent to which they agreed or disagreed with the following statements: sometimes I rather enjoy going against the rules and doing things that I'm not supposed to do; sometimes I will take a risk just for the fun of it; I sometimes find it exciting to do things for which I might get in trouble; excitement and adventure are more important to me than peace and security; I like to take chances; the things I like to do best are dangerous; and, I like to test myself every now and then by doing something a little risky. For this scale, lower values were associated with higher degrees of nonsocial reinforcement. As shown in table 2.5, the reliability for this scale was strong (alpha = .831).

For strain theory, we sought to capture the perceptions by the youths of limited access to legitimate opportunities. We selected five items from our survey for this scale. The items included: even with a good education, people like me will have to work harder to make a living; no matter how hard I work, I will never be given the same opportunities as other kids; I believe that people like me are treated unfairly when it comes to getting a good job; society is against people like me; and, laws are passed to keep people like me from succeeding. For this scale, lower values represent higher levels of strain. From table 2.5, we find that the reliability for this scale is acceptable (alpha = .659).

In the case of control theory, we selected a number of items that captured the concept of school attachment. Four items from the survey were found to provide a scale with an acceptable level of reliability (alpha = .670). The items were as follows: I like school; I find most of my courses interesting; going to school has been an enjoyable experience for me; and, most schoolwork that is given to me is meaningful and important. For this scale, lower values represent higher degrees of school attachment.

Quality of Measurement

In this study, we were able to look at reliability primarily in terms of internal consistency. A number of multi-item scales were included in the survey instrument. The authors found a number of reliable scales in an earlier administration of a similar instrument with a smaller sample (Jarjoura and May 2000). In table 2.5, we present a series of scales of interest, along with assessments of the internal consistency of our survey instrument. Generally, the scales considered here demonstrate acceptable to good levels of internal consistency. For each scale, we present the reliability estimates for the entire sample. As we used alpha coefficients, we were particularly interested in finding coefficients that were equal to or greater than .60, which would reflect acceptable levels of internal consistency. Alphas of .70 or better reflect strong consistency across the various items in that scale. We conducted extensive analyses to determine whether the reliabilities for the indices varied by gender and facility where the respondent was housed. We did not include those analyses here, as there were no substantive differences in the scale reliabilities by either gender or facility.

In addition, we checked the responses to pairs of items for logical consistency. For example, respondents were asked to respond to items "If the cops don't like you, they will get you for anything" and "Police almost always have a good reason when they stop somebody." We would expect opposite responses to these questions. We examined four such pairs. We then scored each person in terms of the number of inconsistencies. Only 9.5% of the sample scored above 2.

To examine the validity of these measures, we consider the correlations between the scales we present here and the outcome measures related to violence. In table 2.4, we examine correlations between the scales and the different measures of violence. We also considered the correlations between factors that have been shown in the literature to be related. We considered a number of such comparisons and found evidence of convergent validity. For example, the correlations between differential association and each of the measures of violent delinquency were positive. That is, higher degrees of susceptibility to the negative influence of peers were associated with higher levels of involvement in violent forms of delinquency. Similarly, the relationship between the other theoretical scales and the outcome measures were in the expected direction consistently. When we consider the associations between the outcome measures and variables that have been shown in previous research to exist, we find the expected patterns to be evident in these data. For instance, the relationship between perceived neighborhood incivilities and violent forms of delinquency is positive and moderately strong in each case. We also find, as expected, a positive association between the perceived risk of victimization and the various measures of violent delinquency. All of this evidence supports a conclusion of validity for these data.

Qualitative Data to Supplement Survey Results

One of the authors of this book also completed a qualitative research study on a group of youths from the highest-security facility for boys in Indiana. As these data were drawn from a subset of the population under examination here and in the same relative time period, we are incorporating some of the qualitative data in this study. Beginning in the fall of 1999, Jarjoura conducted a series of life-history interviews with all of the 18-year-old males in custody at the facility during the month of November 1999. Twenty-five youths participated in the life-history interviews. For each interview, the researcher and the youth met on a series of occasions until the life history was complete. Completed interviews lasted between three hours (the shortest interview) and twelve hours (the longest interview).

The interviews themselves focused on the entire life span of the youth, from birth through age 18. The life of the youth was split into periods: from birth to pre-kindergarten, from kindergarten through the end of elementary school, middle school, and high school. During each phase, the youths were invited to talk about their family, school, neighborhood, and peer experiences. Special attention was paid to events that held significant meaning for the youths and to the quality and nature of relationships with family, peers, and teachers. In addition, significant attention was paid to the involvement of the youth in juvenile delinquency and the juvenile justice system. Of particular interest for this study, questions were posed regarding experiences with gangs, guns, and drugs. Finally, the youths were invited to share their aspirations for the future.

At the completion of the study, transcripts of the interviews were prepared. Excerpts from these transcripts have been selected as representative examples of the issues being examined here. In each of the next chapters, we include several excerpts to supplement the analyses based on the survey data. These narratives add to the richness of the voices of the youths on the issues of guns and violence.

Tables

TABLE 2.1 Prevalence of delinquent activity among full sample

Measure of delinquency	%
Drunk in a public place	61.5
Loud, rowdy, or unruly in a public place	67.4
Gambled illegally	56.8
Paid for having sexual relations with someone	17.0
Drove a car while drunk	43.5
Involved in a gang fight	42.4
Sold marijuana or hashish	60.7
Sold hard drugs such as heroin, cocaine, or LSD	39.3
Knowingly bought, sold, or held something stolen	66.9
Taken a vehicle for a ride without the owner's permission	52.0
Stole or tried to steal things worth between $5 and $50 at school	27.7
Stole or tried to steal things worth between $5 and $50 at places other than school	48.1
Stole or tried to steal things worth more than $50 at school	24.4
Stole or tried to steal things worth more than $50 at places other than school	47.5
Purposely damaged/destroyed property belonging to your school	35.8
Purposely damaged/destroyed property that did not belong to you	48.8
Broke into a building or vehicle	48.6
Stole or tried to steal a motor vehicle	41.3
Used force (strong-arm methods) to get money or things from schoolmates	21.9
Used force (strong-arm methods) to get money or things from people other than family members or schoolmates	26.0
Hit or threatened to hit a schoolmate or teacher at school	67.2
Hit or threatened to hit someone other than a schoolmate, teacher, or family member	64.9
Attacked someone with the idea of seriously hurting or killing him/her	43.2
Had or tried to have sexual relations with someone against their will	13.1
Had alcoholic beverages	74.0
Had marijuana or hashish	75.0
Had hallucinogens	37.3
Had amphetamines	31.6
Had barbiturates	26.4
Had heroin	11.7
Had cocaine	30.4
Had crack	18.1
Used a weapon to commit a crime	43.2
Used a gun to commit a crime	32.0
Carried a gun for protection	40.7

TABLE 2.2 Characteristics of youths in sample

Demographic characteristics	N	%
Age (in years)		
12	2	0.3
13	15	1.9
14	59	7.4
15	159	20.0
16	248	31.2
17	214	26.9
18	84	10.6
19	12	1.5
20	2	0.3
Gender		
Male	662	80.0
Female	166	20.0
Race		
Caucasian	404	49.3
African American	287	35.0
Native American	24	2.9
Latino	30	3.7
Asian	3	0.4
Other	71	8.7
Family structure prior to incarceration		
Both biological parents	151	18.4
Mother only	262	32.0
Father only	63	7.7
One parent and a stepparent	162	19.8
One parent and a grandparent	17	2.1
Grandparents	50	6.1
Other	114	13.9
Biological parents married to one another		
Yes	169	20.8
No	645	79.2
Number of siblings in home		
0	221	27.5
1	235	29.2
2	161	20.0
3	96	11.9
4	46	5.7
5	25	3.1
6 or more	21	2.6
Have any children?		
Yes	135	17.2
No	650	82.8
Length of time at address (in years)		
Less than 1 year	95	12.2
1-2 years	132	16.8
2-3 years	96	12.2
3-5 years	121	15.4
5-10 years	137	17.5
More than 10 years	204	26.0
Family received public assistance		
Yes	245	32.8
No	502	67.2

. . . .

TABLE 2.2 *(continued)*

School experiences	N	%
Last grade in school		
6th	23	2.9
7th	37	4.7
8th	143	18.0
9th	250	31.5
10th	212	26.7
11th	94	11.9
12th	34	4.3
Most recent grade average		
A+	37	4.8
A	55	7.1
A-	30	3.9
B+	57	7.3
B	100	12.9
B-	84	10.8
C+	108	13.9
C	96	12.3
C-	84	10.8
D or below	127	16.3
Highest level of school you would like to finish?		
9th grade	36	4.5
10th grade	17	2.1
11th grade	14	1.8
High school diploma or GED	224	28.2
Vocational or trade school	56	7.1
Some college	55	6.9
College degree	391	49.3
How far will you really get in school?		
9th grade	27	3.4
10th grade	26	3.3
11th grade	40	5.1
High school diploma or GED	297	37.5
Vocational or trade school	72	9.1
Some college	82	10.4
College degree	247	31.2
Ever been suspended?		
Yes	747	94.0
No	48	6.0
Ever been expelled?		
Yes	507	64.3
No	281	35.7
Ever had to repeat a grade?		
Yes	371	46.8
No	421	53.2

TABLE 2.3 Characteristics of respondents' parents

Characteristic	Mother N	Mother %	Father N	Father %
Employment status				
Takes care of house	164	21.3	67	9.1
Employed full time	371	48.2	374	50.7
Employed part time	111	14.4	54	7.3
Retired	10	1.3	33	4.5
Unemployed, looking for work	40	5.2	35	4.7
Other	73	9.5	175	23.7
Occupation				
Manager/Professional	130	15.8	70	9.2
Retail	75	9.1	22	2.9
Government/service	229	27.8	59	7.8
Agricultural	2	0.2	15	2.0
Factory	7	0.8	47	6.2
Maintenance	47	5.7	57	7.5
Shop worker	8	1.0	5	0.7
Construction	4	0.5	166	21.9
Driver/delivery	24	2.9	61	8.0
None	298	36.2	256	33.8
Educational attainment				
8th grade or less	23	2.9	34	6.4
Some high school	156	19.7	125	23.4
Completed high school	257	32.5	217	40.6
Some college	77	9.7	67	12.5
Completed college	151	19.8	91	17.0

TABLE 2.4 Convergent validity between created scales and outcomes of violent offending

	Used Gun to Commit Crime	Committed Violent Crime	Committed Robbery	Committed Aggravated Assault	Participated in Gang Fight
Differential Association	.260	.179	.204	.281	.247
Nonsocial Reinforcement	-.211	-.192	-.211	-.246	-.259
School Attachment	.183	.118	.204	.160	.131
Strain	-.171	-.097	-.209	-.155	-.200
Neighborhood Incivilities	.377	.260	.290	.313	.397
Perceived Risk of Victimization	.229	.174	.218	.189	.199

TABLE 2.5 Descriptive statistics for scales and indexes used in analyses

Scale/Index	Item #	Item from survey	Strongly Agree (%)	Agree (%)	Somewhat Agree (%)	Somewhat Disagree (%)	Disagree (%)	Strongly Disagree (%)	Factor Score	Cronbach's alpha
Neighborhood incivilities										.787
	Q159	I feel safe from crime in my neighborhood	24.1	21.0	19.0	11.8	11.8	12.2	.727	
	Q167	In my neighborhood, people will call the police right away if they think a crime is being committed	22.7	21.1	20.4	10.3	13.2	12.3	.579	
	Q179r	My neighborhood is noisy and the streets always seem to have litter on them	12.4	11.1	15.4	11.3	22.0	27.8	.712	
	Q199r	There are gangs in my neighborhood	33.3	16.6	11.4	7.2	10.3	21.3	.684	
	Q248r	My neighborhood is getting worse all of the time	13.8	11.2	17.2	14.6	20.7	22.5	.727	
	Q262	Most of the people living in my neighborhood are good, upstanding citizens	17.8	21.8	21.9	11.9	11.0	15.7	.752	
Perceived Risk of Victimization										.798
	Q147	have someone break into your house while your family is away?	Mean rating (on scale of 1 to 10) = 2.74						.678	
How LIKELY do you think it is that you will:	Q148	be raped or sexually assaulted?	Mean rating (on scale of 1 to 10) = 2.14						.598	
	Q149	be murdered?	Mean rating (on scale of 1 to 10) = 2.99						.804	
	Q150	be attacked by someone with a weapon?	Mean rating (on scale of 1 to 10) = 3.64						.800	
	Q151	have something that belongs to you taken from you?	Mean rating (on scale of 1 to 10) = 4.62						.557	
	Q152	be robbed or mugged?	Mean rating (on scale of 1 to 10) = 3.47						.800	

TABLE 2.5 (continued)

Scale/Index	Item #	Item from survey	Strongly Agree (%)	Agree (%)	Somewhat Agree (%)	Somewhat Disagree (%)	Disagree (%)	Strongly Disagree (%)	Factor Score	Cronbach's alpha
Differential Association										.741
	Q191	My best friends disapprove of people trying drinks of an alcoholic beverage	10.2	9.7	15.4	12.1	24.3	28.3	.686	
	Q223	Most of the people I associate with would never break the law	7.0	7.4	16.7	15.9	25.1	27.8	.675	
	Q236	My best friends disapprove of people taking illegal drugs occasionally	10.5	10.5	14.6	14.9	24.4	25.2	.750	
	Q297	If I were thinking of breaking the law, my friends would tell me not to do it	13.0	16.2	26.3	16.9	12.3	15.3	.674	
	Q329	My best friend encourages me to continue my education after high school	31.6	23.6	16.9	7.6	9.7	10.6	.501	
	Q357	My best friends disapprove of people smoking one or more packs of cigarettes per day	15.8	15.4	15.8	15.4	19.3	18.5	.566	
School Attachment										.670
	Q206	I like school	20.3	22.5	25.5	8.7	7.4	15.6	.759	
	Q252	I find most of my courses interesting	15.7	23.3	29.4	12.8	9.3	9.5	.602	
	Q296	Going to school has been an enjoyable experience for me	18.9	17.6	28.2	12.6	11.1	11.6	.776	
	Q325	Most school work that is meaningful and important	21.5	25.4	25.1	10.7	7.7	9.7	.690	

TABLE 2.5 (continued)

Scale/Index	Item #	Item from survey	Strongly Agree (%)	Agree (%)	Somewhat Agree (%)	Somewhat Disagree (%)	Disagree (%)	Strongly Disagree (%)	Factor Score	Cronbach's alpha
Nonsocial reinforcement										.831
	Q157	I like to test myself every now and then by doing something a little risky	13.9	23.5	25.5	12.3	13.2	11.7	.609	
	Q208	Excitement and adventure are more important to me than peace and security	12.1	15.4	24.2	16.8	17.6	13.9	.537	
	Q217	I sometimes find it exciting to do things for which I might get in trouble	13.0	20.0	24.8	13.8	16.0	12.4	.807	
	Q222	Sometimes I will take a risk just for the fun of it	18.3	21.8	21.6	10.4	14.3	13.6	.806	
	Q232	I like to take chances	22.8	26.1	28.6	9.6	7.5	5.5	.719	
	Q242	Sometimes I rather enjoy going against the rules and doing things that I'm not supposed to do	14.5	18.7	26.9	12.5	14.2	13.2	.743	
	Q251	The things I like to do best are dangerous	16.4	15.2	22.7	12.4	16.7	16.6	.717	
Strain										.659
	Q162	No matter how hard I work, I will never be given the same opportunities as other kids	8.8	12.1	16.0	11.4	24.1	27.6	.631	
	Q177	I believe that people like me are treated unfairly when it comes to getting a good job	16.5	13.6	22.7	10.9	20.0	16.4	.654	
	Q218	Society is against people like me	17.4	13.6	21.9	13.1	18.3	15.6	.650	
	Q224	Laws are passed to keep people like me from succeeding	9.2	6.4	12.2	16.8	25.8	29.6	.628	
	Q247	Even with a good education, people like me will have to work harder to make a	15.8	18.1	24.3	13.5	13.3	15.0	.620	

CHAPTER 3

Where do Juveniles Obtain Their Guns?

Previous Research on Adolescent Gun Acquisition

The first topic we consider in this analysis is where the youth under study here obtained the firearms that they used or possessed. We begin by reviewing extant research regarding this topic, then turn to the analyses from the present data. In their interviews with sixty-three incarcerated juvenile offenders in Atlanta, Ash et al. (1996) determined that 42% were given their first gun by a peer, relative, or older youth, 5% found their first gun, and 5% obtained their first gun during a robbery or burglary. Almost one in five (17%) borrowed their first gun and one in ten bought (11%) or stole (10%) their first gun.

Birkbeck et al. (1999) determined that almost half (43.8%) of the 380 incarcerated juveniles they interviewed obtained their first gun from a friend, one in five (20.5%) had obtained their first gun from a drug dealer, and about one in seven (14.1%) had received their first gun from a family member. Approximately half (48.4%) of those who received their first gun from a friend and three in five (62.5%) of those who obtained their first gun from a family member were given the gun as a gift. Half (51.7%) of those who obtained their first gun from a drug dealer bought or traded for the gun.

Wright and Rossi (1986) found that most of the members of their sample of adult criminals were unable to obtain a firearm legally even before their incarceration (as they were previously convicted felons), setting the expectation that for this sample, gun acquisition will primarily involve illegal means. Among handgun owners, almost half (43%) obtained their most recent handgun through a cash purchase, thirty-two percent had stolen their most recent handgun, nine percent had rented or borrowed it, seven percent had traded for it, and eight percent had received it as a gift. Sixty percent of the handgun owners reported being able to obtain a handgun within a few hours, once they decided to obtain one. When asked where they obtained their most recent handgun, 40% had obtained it from a friend, 14% had obtained it on the street, and 11% had acquired it from a gun shop.

A significant finding from their analysis is that a vast majority of the offenders (804 out of 949) obtained their most recent handgun from sources that would not be covered by any legislation that exists, either in 1986 or 2005. Even among respondents who owned long guns, only one third had obtained their most recent long gun from a retail outlet, two in three had not. Thus, Wright and Rossi (1986) suggest "regulations imposed at the point of retail sale miss the overwhelming majority of all criminal handgun transactions" (185).

Sheley and Wright (1995) also assessed how respondents would go about obtaining a firearm if they wanted one (see also Smith 1996). Just over half of the sample reported that they would "get one off the street" while forty-five percent stated they would borrow one from a family member or friend. Approximately one in three responded that they would "get one from a drug dealer." An equal number would "get one from a junkie." A similar proportion of the sample reported they would buy one from a family member or friend. Less than one in five (17%) stated that they would steal one from a house or an apartment, while a slightly smaller number (14%) said they would steal one from a person or car. Thus, street sources and informal purchases and trades with family, friends, and acquaintances were the primary means through which the inmates would obtain their firearms (Sheley and Wright 1995).

Smith (1996) notes youths are most likely to acquire a gun by purchasing it. He goes on to show that among juvenile correctional inmates, the second most likely method of acquiring a firearm is through theft. Youths were most likely to be able to purchase or receive a gun from their peer networks. Inmates also turned to people on the streets or those involved with drugs to acquire guns as well. As shown in his analyses, Smith notes that even when they purchase or trade guns from their friends, those guns are very likely to have been stolen at some point prior to the current transfer. Finally, Smith notes that youths are able to acquire guns for relatively small amounts of money. In his sample, more than half of those purchasing a gun paid less than $100.

In a National Institute of Justice survey (U.S. Department of Justice 2000a) of recent arrestees, it was found that the use of guns in criminal activities was higher for juvenile arrestees, for those who were selling drugs, and for those in gangs. Juvenile arrestees were two times as likely as arrestees in general to have stolen a firearm. Theft of a firearm was also found to be more prevalent for gang members and drug dealers among the juvenile arrestee population. Carrying a gun for protection was also related to a higher likelihood of using guns to commit crimes.

The Current Analysis

In our sample, we asked the youths to indicate how they would acquire a gun if they needed to get one. We specifically asked "If I needed to get a gun, I would get one by (check all that apply):" The choices they could select included:

- Buy it from a gun store
- Steal it from a store or shipping truck

- Steal/buy it from a drug dealer
- Steal/buy it from a friend or relative
- Steal it from a car or house
- Steal/buy one from a drug addict
- Borrow one from a friend or relative
- Buy it on the streets
- Other (please indicate how: _____)

Sources of Gun Acquisition

A breakdown of how many youths would elect to use each choice is provided in table 3.1. The most common response among this sample was to buy the gun on the streets. Almost half (44%) of the respondents indicated they would look to buy a gun on the streets if they needed to get one. This was followed closely by borrowing a gun from a friend or relative (41%). Next in popularity was to look to drug addicts as a potential source to purchase or steal a firearm. Friends and relatives were also seen as likely targets for purchase and/or theft.

Nearly one-third of the youths would consider looking to drug dealers as a source to purchase or steal a gun. Nearly one-third of the sample also indicated they would steal a gun from a house or a car if they needed one. The least likely sources for acquiring a gun would be to purchase from a retail store (27%) and to steal it from a store or shipping truck (23%).

We did not ask how the youths actually acquired the guns that they have possessed in the past, although it is reasonable to assume that if they had already used one of the above strategies, they are likely to see that as a means of acquiring another gun in the future. Youths can also speak to available means to acquire guns because of what they have learned from their own informal networks in the community. They may know people that will sell guns on the street. They may know of houses where guns are owned that they may burglarize if they need a gun. It is instructive to consider differences in the proposed methods of gun acquisition based on characteristics of the juvenile offenders.

From the literature, we know that juvenile offenders are more likely to carry guns and use them in the commission of a crime if they are involved in robberies, drug using, drug selling, and aggravated assault. Youths involved in gangs are also more likely to carry guns and use them in the course of a criminal act. In table 3.2, we examine the decision to purchase a gun from a gun store based on differences in the criminal activity and gang involvement of the youths. In this table, we present a summary of the results from a number of contingency table analyses. We report the percentage in each group that indicated they would follow that particular strategy to obtain a firearm.

To assess the relationship between the two variables, we report two different statistics. First, we report a chi-squared test of a contingency table. This statistic provides us with evidence of any association between the independent and dependent variable. We can also examine the strength of the association between the two variables. We report phi for each relationship being examined. Phi is a measure of association for contingency tables that are 2 X 2 in size. Phi tells us about the strength (the magnitude of the number, with stronger relationships being reflected by values close to 1 or -1) and direction (the sign of the statistic) of a relationship between two variables. Phi is a measure of the correlation between two nominal-level measures (Knoke, Bohrnstedt, and Potter Mee 2002).

The most striking finding is that when youths report they will purchase a gun from a retail store, there are no significant differences based on any of the variables we consider here. Regardless of whether the youth has carried a gun for protection, has been involved in a number of violent offenses, has been a gang member, or has used or sold drugs, they seem to be equally likely to have identified a gun store as a likely source of acquiring a firearm. There are also no apparent differences based on gender or race.

On the other hand, when we consider the other potential sources of acquiring guns, we find that many of the variables we are using here predict the various choices the youths can make. In table 3.3, we examine the decision to steal a gun from a gun store or shipping truck, again based on differences in the criminal activity and gang involvement of the youths. Here we find that every variable we consider is a significant predictor of the choice to steal a gun from a retail store or a shipping truck. The results indicate that males are more likely than females to consider stealing a gun from this source as a potential means of acquiring a firearm. White youths are more likely than nonwhite youths to select this strategy. If the youth has engaged in violence in past or has been involved with using or dealing drugs, they are much more likely to see the theft of a gun from a store or shipping truck as a way to get a gun if they needed to have one. The three strongest correlations from this table are for those who have previously engaged in robbery, have carried a gun for protection, or have sold drugs other than marijuana.

In table 3.4, we examine the decision to buy or steal a gun from a drug dealer. We find similar results here as we did in the previous table. Every variable we consider provides us with a significant result, helping us to understand which youths are more likely to make this choice. Again, the three strongest associations are for those youths who have carried a gun for protection, sold drugs other than marijuana, and committed robbery.

In table 3.5, we examine the decision to buy or steal a gun from a friend or relative. As with the two preceding tables, we find similar patterns in the results. Again, the strongest associations are for those youths who have carried a gun for protection and those who have sold drugs other than marijuana. In this set of results, we do not find as strong an effect for having committed robbery in the past.

In table 3.6, we examine the decision to steal a gun from a car or a house. The pattern of results continues to be consistent with the previous tables. We do find stronger associations in this table than the previous tables. It appears that the variables we consider here are particularly effective in distinguishing choices that are clearly criminal. In some of the options available, there is no distinction between buying and stealing from the source. Here, it is clear that we are only looking at the theft of a firearm from a house or a vehicle. These are unambiguously criminal decisions. We find here stronger associations for those who have carried a gun for protection, been a member of a gang, and for those who have been dealing drugs.

In table 3.7, we examine the decision to buy or steal a gun from a drug addict. Here we find the associations to be less strong than in the previous tables. In this set of results, only for those who have previously sold drugs other than marijuana do we achieve a phi of .300 or higher. In addition, in this set of results we found no significant difference based on race in the likelihood of using this strategy.

In table 3.8, we examine the decision to borrow a gun from a friend or a relative. For this set of results, while every association considered is statistically significant, none of them achieve a phi of .300 or higher. Consistent with the findings from above, the strongest associations were found for those who have carried a gun for protection and for those who have been involved in selling and using drugs.

In table 3.9, we examine the decision to buy a gun from someone on the streets. Some of the strongest effects from this section of the analysis are to be found in this set of results. Consistent with results from above, those who carried a gun for protection, those who have ever been a member of a gang, and those who have sold drugs in the past are all significantly more likely to consider buying a gun from someone on the streets. As we have seen in some of the tables in this chapter so far, there is no significant difference between the racial subgroups on this strategy for acquiring a firearm.

Gun Acquisition among those Who have Used Guns to Commit Crimes

It is perhaps more instructive to consider the sources of acquiring firearms for those who have already made the choice to use a gun to commit a crime. These results are presented in tables 3.10-3.18. Table 3.10 provides us with a summary view of the prevalence of each choice among the group of youths who have used a gun to commit a crime in the past. We refer to these youths as gun criminals. Additionally, we asked the respondents that admitted they had used a gun in crime an open-ended question asking them what type of gun they had used in crime (discussed in detail in chapter 5). Responses were categorized into five categories: small-caliber handguns, medium-caliber handguns, large-caliber handguns, shotguns, and automatic or semi-automatic gun. Contingency analyses are estimated for these variables as well.

The results in this table are consistent with the results we presented above in table 3.1. The most likely source for acquiring guns is still to buy from someone on the streets. Nearly three-fourths (71%) of the sample would use this strategy. In contrast, relatively few (only 26%) of the gun criminals would try to buy a gun from a gun store. As before, we examine the individual options one by one.

In table 3.11, we examine the decision to buy a gun from a gun store. Among gun criminals, nonwhites are significantly more likely than whites to look to a gun store as a source for acquiring a gun. This suggests, perhaps, that the two groups have different experiences or expectations (based on informal networks, for instance) about the likelihood of being able to purchase a firearm from a retail store. We are unable to explore this possibility further with our data. The only other significant difference in the decision to buy from a gun store has to do with the previous use of a medium-caliber handgun. Those who have previously used a medium-caliber handgun to commit a crime are significantly less likely to consider buying a gun from a gun store.

In table 3.12, we examine the decision to steal a gun from a store or a shipping truck. Among gun criminals, males are significantly more likely to select this strategy than females, and whites are significantly more likely to select this approach than nonwhites. Gun criminals are also significantly more likely to select this method of acquiring guns if they have previously engaged in robbery or have been selling or using drugs other than marijuana.

In table 3.13, we examine the decision to buy or steal a gun from a drug dealer. There are a number of factors here that would make it more likely that a gun criminal would select this method for acquiring a handgun. Male gun criminals are more likely to take this approach than female gun criminals are. Also, among gun criminals, whites are more likely than nonwhites to select this method. As we have come to expect from the previous results, previous involvement in selling drugs, robbery, and aggravated assault are all significantly related to the choice to buy or steal a gun from a drug dealer. Similarly, having carried a gun for protection, used a weapon to commit a crime, and taken part in a gang fight all make it more likely that a gun criminal will take this approach to obtaining a firearm.

In table 3.14, we examine the decision to buy or steal a gun from a friend or relative. Such a choice is more likely for those who have carried a gun for protection or used a weapon to commit a crime in the past. We also find that gun criminals are more likely to select this approach if they have previously committed an aggravated assault or if they have sold drugs other than marijuana.

In table 3.15, we examine the decision to steal a gun from a car or house. Males are more likely to choose this approach, as are whites. In addition, among gun criminals with previous involvement in selling or using drugs other than marijuana, there is a significantly higher likelihood of choosing to acquire a gun in this way. Finally, if a gun criminal previously used a small-caliber handgun to commit a crime, they are more likely to choose this approach to getting a gun.

In table 3.16, we examine the decision to buy or steal a gun from a drug addict. Among drug criminals, we find there are not very many differences in the likelihood of selecting this method. It is one of the least prevalent sources of acquiring a gun (see table 3.10) and we find no strong associations to help predict the likelihood of making this choice. Two significant differences stand out. First, those gun criminals who were previously involved in selling drugs other than marijuana were more likely to choose this approach to obtaining a gun.

Also, if a gun criminal used a shotgun in the past to commit a crime, then he or she is more likely to see drug addicts as a potential source for getting a gun.

In table 3.17, we examine the decision to borrow a gun from a friend or relative. Among gun criminals, whites are more likely than nonwhites to use this approach. In addition, previous involvement in using or selling drugs, regardless of the type, is significantly associated with a higher likelihood for choosing this approach to obtaining a gun. Finally, those gun criminals who have used a shotgun to commit a crime are more likely to try and borrow a gun from a friend or relative.

In table 3.18, we examine the decision to buy a gun from someone on the street. This is the most popular strategy for acquiring a gun among the subsample of gun criminals, and there are a number of factors that significantly distinguish whether or not a person would select this strategy. Males are more likely to take this approach, as are whites. If the gun criminal has carried a gun for protection or has used a small-caliber or medium-caliber handgun to commit crimes in the past, they are more likely to choose to buy a gun from someone on the streets. Similarly, if they have previously used an automatic or semi-automatic gun or a shotgun in the commission of a crime, they are more likely to try and buy a gun on the streets. Selling drugs, gang membership, and taking part in a gang fight are also related to the choice to buy a gun from someone on the streets.

Qualitative Data

From the life-history narrative data that we have available, we can put more of a human face on the choices that youths make when they are trying to obtain a gun. In the following excerpt, Rodney talks about how he was able to acquire and then get rid of a handgun. This provides some insights into the informal networks that lend themselves to the easy access of firearms for teenagers.

Did you ever own a gun?
Rodney: Yeah, I had a little .22 handgrip. I bought it. Actually, I traded a pager to R____ for it.
For a gun?
Rodney: Yeah, he wanted a pager. He had robbed this dude's house—him and J____ had robbed this dude's house for all kind of guns. He had like five or six guns. Some rifles, sniper rifles, shotguns, and handguns. So he just, um, he wanted a pager so I had the extra pager and I wanted a gun and he had the gun so we just traded.
What did you want a gun for?
Rodney: Just to have a gun. Actually I was wanting like do target practice, like a sign or whatever, you know. Just to shoot a gun, cause I think guns are pretty cool, if they're in the right hands anyway. I just wanted to do like shoot at a sign, but I only shot it like twice. I ended up selling it for twenty-five dollars to my friend in Lafayette named T____.
Why did you sell it?
Rodney: Just to have, actually it wasn't even my idea to sell it. He was like,

"you want to sell that?" I was like, "how much you gonna give me for it?" He was like, "I'll give twenty-five for it." I was like, "yeah, sure you know I want twenty-five dollars." So I think he just bought it just to get it out of my hands. Cause he was older and more mature. He was like, "he don't need it." He ended up getting rid of it like two days after he bought it from me. So he didn't want it too. He didn't buy it 'cause he wanted it. I'm pretty sure he bought it just to get it out of my hands.

Another youth, Casper tells us

In sixth grade I bought my first gun.
You bought it?
Yeah, on the street market.
How did you have money to buy a gun?
I took it from my uncle to give to the neighbor or something and they would give me money for doing the favor and I would save it up. Then when I got $150, I bought my first gun. My first gun was a .25, it was little.
What did you do with it?
I carried it with me.

Guy discussed the kinds of guns he and his friends were able to obtain on the streets.

They pull out their guns we pull our guns, they had little .25's and stuff like that we had tech 9's, Uzi's, .40 cals, .50 cals, we had all that.
How did you guys have those guns?
We just bought them off the street.

Another youth, Corey, tells how he was able to get guns on the streets:

How did you get these guns?
People on the streets.
Did you buy them?
(Nods.)
Did you ever steal a gun?
Yes. I stole a sawed-off shotgun.
From whom?
Some guy on the streets. I went to buy it. I gave him the money and the dummy left a bullet in there. There was a bullet in the chamber so I pumped it and got right to his face and said, "Give me my money back." I said, "Put my money on the ground and run." He threw it on the ground and ran. I got my money back and walked away. I put the sawed off up and ran home.
We call that a robbery.
Well he tried to sell it to me. He was selling to a minor. He was like 30. You should've seen the look on his face.

In another excerpt, Corey notes that being in a gang also helps with access to guns:

So are there other bad things about being in a gang?
The bad things that if you are told to do something you got to do it or you will suffer the consequences. You take your violations. The good things are that you've got connections. You can get just about anything. Like I had my hands on a lot of different kinds of guns.

Another youth, Scott, who never actually owned a gun, was able to carry a gun because his friends provided him with the access:

I've shot a gun with my dad but I've carried a gun with my friends and stuff.
How did you get that gun?
It was a friend's of mine.
Then why were you carrying it?
Just 'cause I wanted.

Grant describes a time that he stole a gun with another friend:

We stole a AK-47 assault rifle one time. We stole it from this, uh, kid's brother that was in the Army. He'd, uh, been in the Army. We'd known that he had a AK-47 downstairs so we waited for the parents to leave and everybody was at work. We broke the window out and stole it

Grant goes on to talk about other guns he was able to get through trading with his "clients":

I sold a little bit of drugs in my time. So I'd have people come without money and, you know, they'd say, hey I got this or I'd give 'em drugs and they'd give me that. Or, I'd break into some houses and find a bunch of guns. I had a bunch of shotguns that me and my friends stole and we sold 'em the next day for like 300 bucks for the bunch of 'em. We just got rid of 'em 'cause you can't use shotguns. We always kept the handguns.

A similar situation is evident in the narrative provided by Marvin:

How many guns have you ever owned? Do you know?
All together, probably about close to 100. I used to collect guns a lot and sell 'em just to make money.
So what kinds of guns are you talking about?
I had machine guns, shotguns, pistols, everything, basically.
How did a kid get guns like that?
Just from people.
Just from people? What do you mean?
I had, I had a bunch of, I had a Tech-9 that someone stole and brought to me. I don't know how people get 'em. You know what I'm sayin', I get 'em from people that bring 'em to me and they want money. So I buy 'em from them and then I sell 'em to somebody else.

And how did you have the money to buy guns?
From sellin' drugs. I've stole a lot of guns, too. I mean, if I know somebody
that has a lot a stolen guns, I mean that's kinda stupid but, then I'll just take
'em from them, if I don't like 'em. That's how I got a lot of my stuff.

Another youth, Ignis, describes a family connection that he was able to use to
obtain a gun:

Have you ever owned a gun?
Yes I have.
What kind of gun?
A .45 Magnum.
How did you get it?
My stepdad.
Was it his gun or your gun?
It's more my gun, I have a permit, but it's more of a forged permit.
How did you do that?
He was an ex-owner of a gun shop.
So he got you this gun illegally?
Well, kind of.

Another family connection is evident in the following example related by J.R.:

Have you ever owned a gun?
Yep.
How did you get it?
I got it from my cousin and he got it from a dude that use to be up here. I took it
from my cousin
You took it from him?
Yes.
You stole it from him?
No, I took it. I was like, "Give it to me," and I didn't give it back to him.
What kind of a gun was it?
It was a 380.
So how long did you have it for?
About three weeks.
Did you use it for anything?
Nope.
Just carried it around?
Yeah, all the time.

One youth, Edmundo, related how he was able to obtain guns by stealing them
from his father:

How many guns would you say you've owned?
Like three or four.
How did you get them?

My first gun I stole from my dad. My first two guns.
Did he notice?
He thought they were missing, he was going crazy looking for them. He put out reports on them for theft, cause if something happened, like if someone killed somebody with them it would come back on him.
Were they registered to him?
Yeah.
You stole them from your father?
Yep. I was like 13 or 14 years old and had a .38 special, then I had a 380. Then I couldn't keep stealing them from him, I mean he would show me, look what I bought, he would show me the gun. I don't ever want you to touch this, but look at it. He said if anything ever happened in the house and he couldn't do anything, he showed me how to cock and load it, and I'm sitting there thinking in my mind, I know how to do this.

For some youths, owning a gun means that they had a gun in their possession for a short period of time. Kane provides an example:

Have you ever owned a gun?
Yeah.
How did you get it?
Well this dude named J____, he moved up from Indianapolis when I was living in Carmel. This dude tried to mess with him so he got his grandpa's .25. I can't remember if it was a .25 or a 9 mm. I know it held 10 bullets and it was about this long. I think it was either a 9 mm Berretta or a .25, but he owned 10 shots and there was one in the chamber and like three bullets in the clip so he couldn't keep it at his house 'cause his mom would know whose it was or she would find it or something. So I kept it at my house. So then I tried to sell it to my boy down beneath.

One of the youths interviewed, Ed, discussed the different ways he got guns:

Now how would you get the guns?
Man, you can get guns from the little things, like shooting dice. You can get a gun for shooting dice. I don't know. Crack feens, they will give you a gun.

We end the chapter with an excerpt from an interview with Michael who describes an incident where he stole a gun from a gun store:

But before right before I moved I went to get my hair cut with my grandfather and right next to it was a gun store and I was like can I go over here and look in this gun store while he was getting his hair cut and he was like yeah. So I went over there and I was looking it was a real small shop and I walked in and was looking around and there was this case on top of the case that was mounted into the ground and the back of it was open but it was facing that way and then there was like a little opening here and I walked around to it and looking and stuff and everything and I looked into it and there was all kinds of real nice guns and stuff. I picked one up and was looking at it and cocked it back and everything, looking at it, set it back down then I seen this 380 and it was nice so I picked it up and looked at it, I looked around and nobody was watching so I stuffed it in my pants. Then I picked up another gun that was next to it and looked at it and set it like in the middle so it looked like a gun wasn't missing. So I was looking around and then my grandfather came in and he was like are you ready to go and I was like yeah. We walked out the store and he took me to Burger King after that. I went to Burger King and I was like paranoid at that.

Why?

I was looking in the rearview mirror to see if somebody was following me or something you know. So we went to Burger King right and he got me like I can't remember two whoppers or something. I was sitting there eating them right and then I was like I've got to go to the bathroom cause you know I wanted to go look at it. I walked in there and I like got up to go and I turned around and it fell and I was like damn so I reached down and I grabbed it and I held it like right there and I walked back to the bathroom. I pulled it out and everything and I was sitting there right and I took a piss in the toilet right and stuff and I was sitting there and I was looking at it and I hit the button for the clip and the clip fell in the toilet and I was like oh damn. I was like shit I had to reach down there with piss in the toilet and everything and grab it man. I whipped it off and everything and washed my hands and then I had to like try to position it to where it wouldn't fall out. So I went back out and I only ate like half of my hamburger cause I wanted to hurry up and get home.

Tables

TABLE 3.1 Sources of gun acquisition for all respondents

	Yes		No	
If I needed to get a gun I would get one by ...	N	%	N	%
Buy it on the streets	364	44.0	464	56.0
Borrow one from a friend or relative	340	41.1	488	58.9
Steal/buy one from a drug addict	294	35.5	534	64.5
Steal/buy it from a friend or relative	273	33.0	555	67.0
Steal it from a car or house	258	31.2	570	68.8
Steal/buy it from a drug dealer	248	30.0	580	70.0
Buy it from a gun store	227	27.4	601	72.6
Steal it from a store or shipping truck	189	22.8	639	77.2

TABLE 3.2 Analysis of whether respondent would buy a gun from a gun store

Predictor	Yes (%)	No (%)	χ^2	Phi
Male	28.9	21.7	3.424	.064
Nonwhite	28.4	26.5	.390	.022
Family received public assistance	32.2	33.0	.045	-.008
Experienced personal victimization	73.1	79.7	4.052*	-.071*
Carried a gun for protection	27.4	28.5	.128	-.013
Previously committed simple assault	63.5	65.5	.281	-.019
Previously committed aggravated assault	27.8	29.5	.295	-.020
Previously involved in a gang fight	25.8	29.8	1.440	-.043
Previously used weapon to commit crime	25.3	28.7	1.195	-.038
Previously engaged in robbery	25.7	28.1	.469	-.024
Currently or ever been a gang member	25.4	28.5	.938	-.034
Previously sold marijuana	25.5	29.9	1.938	-.048
Previously sold drugs other than marijuana	26.3	28.1	.292	-.019
Previously used marijuana	28.1	25.9	.400	.022
Previously used drugs other than marijuana	29.2	25.9	1.128	.037

* $p < .05$

TABLE 3.3 Analysis of whether respondent would steal a gun from a store or shipping truck

Predictor	Yes (%)	No (%)	χ^2	Phi
Male	27.6	3.6	43.502*	.229*
Nonwhite	18.3	27.7	10.249*	-.112*
Family received public assistance	31.8	33.1	.103	-.012
Experienced personal victimization	85.0	75.7	7.297*	.096*
Carried a gun for protection	40.6	11.8	88.577*	.333*
Previously committed simple assault	81.6	59.7	29.662*	.196*
Previously committed aggravated assault	36.7	14.3	52.312*	.260*
Previously involved in a gang fight	36.8	14.3	52.655*	.260*
Previously used weapon to commit crime	36.6	2.7	64.391*	.281*
Previously engaged in robbery	46.0	13.5	101.151*	.350*
Currently or ever been a gang member	35.5	15.7	42.348*	.226*
Previously sold marijuana	33.2	9.2	66.300*	.283*
Previously sold drugs other than marijuana	41.8	11.8	97.926*	.344*
Previously used marijuana	28.1	10.5	30.230*	.191*
Previously used drugs other than marijuana	36.1	11.0	73.670*	.298*

* p < .05

TABLE 3.4 Analysis of whether respondent would buy or steal a gun from a drug dealer

Predictor	Yes (%)	No (%)	χ^2	Phi
Male	33.8	14.5	23.756*	.169*
Nonwhite	26.3	34.2	6.055*	-.086*
Family received public assistance	33.5	32.5	.070	.010
Experienced personal victimization	83.4	75.4	6.394*	.089*
Carried a gun for protection	50.5	17.5	97.647*	.350*
Previously committed simple assault	80.8	57.6	39.600*	.226*
Previously committed aggravated assault	47.8	19.5	69.886*	.300*
Previously involved in a gang fight	44.7	21.5	47.443*	.247*
Previously used weapon to commit crime	45.2	19.0	64.810*	.282*
Previously engaged in robbery	51.9	21.2	76.230*	.303*
Currently or ever been a gang member	46.8	20.4	63.491*	.277*
Previously sold marijuana	41.7	14,5	71.538*	.294*
Previously sold drugs other than marijuana	51.0	17.7	101.308*	.350*
Previously used marijuana	36.3	15.0	37.609*	.213*
Previously used drugs other than marijuana	44.0	17.4	69.586*	.290*

* p < .05

TABLE 3.5 Analysis of whether respondent would buy or steal a gun from friend or relative

Predictor	Yes (%)	No (%)	χ^2	Phi
Male	36.6	18.7	19.201*	.152*
Nonwhite	28.9	37.4	6.619*	-.090*
Family received public assistance	31.9	33.3	.141	-.014
Experienced personal victimization	84.6	74.4	10.771*	.116*
Carried a gun for protection	53.5	20.7	92.355*	.340*
Previously committed simple assault	80.4	56.6	43.915*	.238*
Previously committed aggravated assault	50.7	23.2	63.440*	.286*
Previously involved in a gang fight	48.0	24.6	45.961*	.243*
Previously used weapon to commit crime	47.4	22.5	56.225*	.263*
Previously engaged in robbery	48.9	26.6	38.338*	.215*
Currently or ever been a gang member	49.5	23.6	57.844*	.264*
Previously sold marijuana	45.1	17.0	72.436*	.296*
Previously sold drugs other than marijuana	53.6	21.0	92.663*	.335*
Previously used marijuana	39.9	16.6	42.692*	.227*
Previously used drugs other than marijuana	45.8	21.5	55.000*	.258*

* p < .05

TABLE 3.6 Analysis of whether respondent would steal a gun from a car or house

Predictor	Yes (%)	No (%)	χ^2	Phi
Male	36.6	9.6	44.830*	.233*
Nonwhite	27.2	35.6	6.732*	-.091*
Family received public assistance	33.6	32.4	.106	.012
Experienced personal victimization	83.2	75.3	6.266*	.089*
Carried a gun for protection	54.5	16.7	126.056*	.397*
Previously committed simple assault	79.9	57.7	37.184*	.219*
Previously committed aggravated assault	47.5	21.6	57.780*	.273*
Previously involved in a gang fight	46.8	21.5	55.690*	.268*
Previously used weapon to commit crime	46.9	19.7	68.774*	.290*
Previously engaged in robbery	52.7	22.5	72.109*	.295*
Currently or ever been a gang member	50.8	20.0	84.473*	.319*
Previously sold marijuana	44.0	14.2	84.111*	.319*
Previously sold drugs other than marijuana	53.3	18.3	109.674*	.364*
Previously used marijuana	37.7	15.8	38.767*	.216*
Previously used drugs other than marijuana	45.5	18.3	71.268*	.293*

* p < .05

TABLE 3.7 Analysis of whether respondent would buy or steal a gun from a drug addict

Predictor	Yes (%)	No (%)	χ^2	Phi
Male	38.5	23.5	13.085*	.126*
Nonwhite	34.0	37.4	1.032	-.035
Family received public assistance	32.7	32.8	.001	-.001
Experienced personal victimization	86.3	73.0	19.071*	.154*
Carried a gun for protection	52.9	24.5	63.031*	.281*
Previously committed simple assault	77.2	57.6	30.737*	.199*
Previously committed aggravated assault	51.0	26.8	47.736*	.248*
Previously involved in a gang fight	49.8	27.3	41.427*	.231*
Previously used weapon to commit crime	47.7	26.8	38.157*	.216*
Previously engaged in robbery	48.9	30.1	26.183*	.178*
Currently or ever been a gang member	50.8	26.8	48.022*	.241*
Previously sold marijuana	46.6	20.9	58.366*	.266*
Previously sold drugs other than marijuana	54.9	24.2	79.169*	.309*
Previously used marijuana	42.2	19.8	37.741*	.213*
Previously used drugs other than marijuana	45.5	26.5	32.462*	.198*

* p < .05

TABLE 3.8 Analysis of whether respondent would borrow gun from friend or relative

Predictor	Yes (%)	No (%)	χ^2	Phi
Male	42.9	33.7	4.607*	.075*
Nonwhite	35.9	46.8	9.995*	-.110*
Family received public assistance	32.8	32.8	.000	.000
Experienced personal victimization	85.8	72.1	21.142*	.163*
Carried a gun for protection	60.0	30.2	69.913*	.296*
Previously committed simple assault	76.2	56.4	32.897*	.206*
Previously committed aggravated assault	55.5	34.1	35.571*	.214*
Previously involved in a gang fight	57.1	32.7	46.328*	.244*
Previously used weapon to commit crime	54.3	31.5	42.593*	.229*
Previously engaged in robbery	57.0	34.7	34.682*	.205*
Currently or ever been a gang member	59.2	30.8	63.595*	.277*
Previously sold marijuana	52.6	26.0	59.303*	.268*
Previously sold drugs other than marijuana	59.9	30.2	70.196*	.291*
Previously used marijuana	50.1	19.8	65.524*	.281*
Previously used drugs other than marijuana	55.5	28.1	63.794*	.278*

* p < .05

TABLE 3.9 Analysis of whether respondent would buy gun from someone on the streets

Predictor	Yes (%)	No (%)	χ^2	Phi
Male	47.7	28.9	19.079*	.152*
Nonwhite	41.9	46.8	1.955	-.049
Family received public assistance	29.9	35.2	2.371	-.056
Experienced personal victimization	83.5	73.2	12.200*	.124*
Carried a gun for protection	68.9	29.6	120.085*	.388*
Previously committed simple assault	78.1	53.6	50.677*	.256*
Previously committed aggravated assault	63.0	33.9	64.845*	.289*
Previously involved in a gang fight	63.5	33.1	70.582*	.302*
Previously used weapon to commit crime	61.4	31.5	72.075*	.297*
Previously engaged in robbery	63.3	36.2	50.360*	.247*
Currently or ever been a gang member	68.6	30.1	114.968*	.373*
Previously sold marijuana	59.4	23.7	104.652*	.356*
Previously sold drugs other than marijuana	65.5	31.5	90.128*	.330*
Previously used marijuana	52.7	23.5	59.929*	.269*
Previously used drugs other than marijuana	58.3	31.1	61.931*	.273*

* $p < .05$

TABLE 3.10 Sources of gun acquisition for gun criminals

If I needed to get a gun I would get one by ...	Yes (N)	%	No (N)	%
Buy it on the streets	188	70.9	77	29.1
Borrow one from a friend or relative	168	63.4	97	36.6
Steal it from a car or house	152	57.4	113	42.6
Steal/buy it from a friend or relative	151	57.0	114	43.0
Steal/buy it from a drug dealer	146	55.1	119	44.9
Steal/buy one from a drug addict	144	54.3	121	45.7
Steal it from a store or shipping truck	120	45.3	145	54.7
Buy it from a gun store	69	26.0	196	74.0

TABLE 3.11 Analysis of whether gun criminals would buy a gun from a store

Predictor	Yes (%)	No (%)	χ^2	Phi
Male	27.1	16.0	1.444	.074
Nonwhite	32.0	17.3	7.266*	.166*
Family received public assistance	32.2	30.6	.051	.014
Experienced personal victimization	70.1	85.6	7.998*	-.175*
Carried a gun for protection	25.5	27.8	.118	-.021
Previously committed simple assault	83.3	81.9	.073	.017
Previously committed aggravated assault	28.6	17.3	3.607	.118
Previously involved in a gang fight	26.3	23.9	.155	.025
Previously used weapon to commit crime	24.5	30.5	.859	-.057
Previously engaged in robbery	26.0	26.1	.000	.000
Used small caliber gun to commit crime	20.4	29.1	2.340	-.094
Used medium caliber gun to commit crime	19.4	38.9	11.687*	-.210*
Used large caliber gun to commit crime	28.0	24.7	.373	.037
Used automatic gun to commit crime	20.6	27.9	1.411	-.073
Used shotgun to commit crime	24.6	26.5	.086	-.018
Currently or ever been a gang member	24.7	28.7	.490	-.043
Previously sold marijuana	25.0	32.4	.913	-.059
Previously sold drugs other than marijuana	26.4	25.3	.042	.013
Previously used marijuana	24.4	34.1	1.777	-.082
Previously used drugs other than marijuana	25.6	26.9	.053	-.014

* $p < .05$

TABLE 3.12 Analysis of whether gun criminals would steal gun from a store or shipping truck

Predictor	Yes (%)	No (%)	χ^2	Phi
Male	48.8	12.0	12.341*	.216*
Nonwhite	36.6	58.2	12.013*	-.214*
Family received public assistance	27.8	33.6	.949	-.062
Experienced personal victimization	86.4	77.8	3.253	.111
Carried a gun for protection	48.1	35.2	2.874	.105
Previously committed simple assault	85.5	79.6	1.525	.077
Previously committed aggravated assault	48.6	37.3	2.757	.103
Previously involved in a gang fight	48.4	38.0	2.223	.093
Previously used weapon to commit crime	48.0	37.3	2.132	.090
Previously engaged in robbery	56.2	31.9	15.537*	.242*
Used small caliber gun to commit crime	52.7	41.3	3.171	.109
Used medium caliber gun to commit crime	48.0	40.0	1.535	.076
Used large caliber gun to commit crime	49.5	42.4	1.308	.070
Used automatic gun to commit crime	48.5	44.2	.389	.038
Used shotgun to commit crime	54.1	42.6	2.485	.097
Currently or ever been a gang member	43.8	48.3	.468	-.042
Previously sold marijuana	46.5	37.8	.962	.060
Previously sold drugs other than marijuana	52.9	30.8	11.783*	.211*
Previously used marijuana	47.1	36.4	1.694	.080
Previously used drugs other than marijuana	50.6	35.5	5.553*	.145*

* $p < .05$

TABLE 3.13 Analysis of whether gun criminals would buy or steal gun from drug dealer

Predictor	Yes (%)	No (%)	χ^2	Phi
Male	57.1	36.0	4.068*	.124*
Nonwhite	47.7	65.5	8.143*	-.176*
Family received public assistance	32.6	29.2	.324	.036
Experienced personal victimization	83.4	79.5	.679	.051
Carried a gun for protection	58.7	42.6	4.475*	.131*
Previously committed simple assault	86.8	76.5	4.629*	.134*
Previously committed aggravated assault	60.0	45.3	4.654*	.134*
Previously involved in a gang fight	55.9	53.5	.119	.022
Previously used weapon to commit crime	59.8	40.7	6.779*	.161*
Previously engaged in robbery	61.0	47.9	4.520*	.131*
Used small caliber gun to commit crime	62.4	51.2	3.062	.107
Used medium caliber gun to commit crime	57.1	51.1	.874	.057
Used large caliber gun to commit crime	57.0	53.8	.266	.032
Used automatic gun to commit crime	63.2	52.3	2.450	.096
Used shotgun to commit crime	62.3	52.9	1.661	.079
Currently or ever been a gang member	55.6	54.0	.060	.015
Previously sold marijuana	57.0	43.2	2.441	.096
Previously sold drugs other than marijuana	61.5	42.9	8.389*	.178*
Previously used marijuana	57.0	45.5	1.982	.086
Previously used drugs other than marijuana	61.6	43.0	8.456*	.179*

* $p < .05$

TABLE 3.14 Analysis of whether gun criminals would buy or steal gun from friend or relative

Predictor	Yes (%)	No (%)	χ^2	Phi
Male	56.7	60.0	.103	-.020
Nonwhite	52.3	63.6	3.363	-.113
Family received public assistance	30.5	31.7	.043	-.013
Experienced personal victimization	84.0	78.6	1.263	.069
Carried a gun for protection	60.6	44.4	4.559*	.132*
Previously committed simple assault	87.3	75.2	6.332*	.156*
Previously committed aggravated assault	63.2	45.3	7.031*	.164*
Previously involved in a gang fight	60.2	49.3	2.503	.099
Previously used weapon to commit crime	60.8	45.8	4.224*	.127*
Previously engaged in robbery	60.3	52.9	1.438	.074
Used small caliber gun to commit crime	60.2	55.2	.611	.048
Used medium caliber gun to commit crime	60.0	51.1	1.916	.085
Used large caliber gun to commit crime	57.9	56.3	.068	.016
Used automatic gun to commit crime	52.9	58.4	.609	-.048
Used shotgun to commit crime	65.6	54.4	2.387	.095
Currently or ever been a gang member	59.0	52.9	.892	.058
Previously sold marijuana	58.8	45.9	2.136	.090
Previously sold drugs other than marijuana	64.4	42.9	11.279*	.206*
Previously used marijuana	59.3	45.5	2.860	.104
Previously used drugs other than marijuana	61.0	49.5	3.304	.112

* $p < .05$

TABLE 3.15 Analysis of whether gun criminals would steal a gun from a car or house

Predictor	Yes (%)	No (%)	χ^2	Phi
Male	59.6	36.0	5.149*	.139*
Nonwhite	49.7	68.2	8.966*	-.185*
Family received public assistance	32.6	28.8	.399	.040
Experienced personal victimization	82.7	80.4	.229	.030
Carried a gun for protection	59.6	48.1	2.303	.094
Previously committed simple assault	83.9	80.0	.656	.050
Previously committed aggravated assault	59.5	52.0	1.214	.068
Previously involved in a gang fight	60.2	47.9	3.183	.111
Previously used weapon to commit crime	59.8	49.2	2.124	.090
Previously engaged in robbery	61.6	52.1	2.441	.096
Used small caliber gun to commit crime	66.7	52.3	5.076*	.138*
Used medium caliber gun to commit crime	58.9	54.4	.473	.042
Used large caliber gun to commit crime	59.8	55.7	.442	.041
Used automatic gun to commit crime	60.3	56.3	.322	.035
Used shotgun to commit crime	65.6	54.9	2.187	.091
Currently or ever been a gang member	57.9	56.3	.057	.015
Previously sold marijuana	59.2	45.9	2.290	.093
Previously sold drugs other than marijuana	64.4	44.0	10.178*	.196*
Previously used marijuana	59.7	45.5	3.057	.107
Previously used drugs other than marijuana	62.2	48.4	4.715*	.133*

* $p < .05$

TABLE 3.16 Analysis of whether gun criminals would buy or steal gun from drug addict

Predictor	Yes (%)	No (%)	χ^2	Phi
Male	54.2	56.0	.031	-.011
Nonwhite	52.3	57.3	.641	-.049
Family received public assistance	29.9	32.4	.189	-.028
Experienced personal victimization	85.9	76.7	3.718	.119
Carried a gun for protection	56.7	44.4	2.607	.100
Previously committed simple assault	85.1	78.8	1.742	.082
Previously committed aggravated assault	57.8	45.3	3.362	.114
Previously involved in a gang fight	57.0	45.1	2.936	.107
Previously used weapon to commit crime	57.8	44.1	3.505	.115
Previously engaged in robbery	55.5	52.9	.170	.025
Used small caliber gun to commit crime	62.4	50.0	3.720	.118
Used medium caliber gun to commit crime	55.4	52.2	.246	.030
Used large caliber gun to commit crime	58.9	51.3	1.490	.075
Used automatic gun to commit crime	61.8	51.8	2.033	.088
Used shotgun to commit crime	67.2	50.5	5.293*	.141*
Currently or ever been a gang member	54.5	54.0	.005	.004
Previously sold marijuana	55.7	45.9	1.221	.068
Previously sold drugs other than marijuana	59.2	45.1	4.815*	.135*
Previously used marijuana	56.6	43.2	2.647	.100
Previously used drugs other than marijuana	55.8	51.6	.429	.040

* $p < .05$

TABLE 3.17 Analysis of whether gun criminals would borrow gun from friend or relative

Predictor	Yes (%)	No (%)	χ^2	Phi
Male	63.3	64.0	.004	-.004
Nonwhite	56.2	72.7	7.500*	-.169*
Family received public assistance	31.6	30.0	.069	.017
Experienced personal victimization	84.9	76.0	3.218	.111
Carried a gun for protection	65.9	55.6	1.972	.087
Previously committed simple assault	86.7	74.2	6.431*	.158*
Previously committed aggravated assault	65.9	58.7	1.225	.069
Previously involved in a gang fight	65.1	60.6	.449	.042
Previously used weapon to commit crime	67.2	52.5	4.236	.127
Previously engaged in robbery	65.1	61.3	.392	.038
Used small caliber gun to commit crime	69.9	59.9	2.606	.099
Used medium caliber gun to commit crime	66.3	57.8	1.854	.084
Used large caliber gun to commit crime	66.4	61.4	.677	.051
Used automatic gun to commit crime	67.6	61.9	.712	.052
Used shotgun to commit crime	75.4	59.8	4.928*	.136*
Currently or ever been a gang member	66.3	57.5	1.959	.086
Previously sold marijuana	65.8	48.6	4.031*	.123*
Previously sold drugs other than marijuana	67.8	54.9	4.266*	.127*
Previously used marijuana	67.4	43.2	9.290*	.187*
Previously used drugs other than marijuana	68.6	53.8	5.729*	.147*

* $p < .05$

TABLE 3.18 Analysis of whether gun criminals would buy gun from someone on the streets

Predictor	Yes (%)	No (%)	χ^2	Phi
Male	73.3	48.0	7.049*	.163*
Nonwhite	66.0	79.1	5.369*	-.143*
Family received public assistance	30.7	31.9	.033	-.012
Experienced personal victimization	84.5	74.7	3.453	.115
Carried a gun for protection	75.0	59.3	5.241*	.141*
Previously committed simple assault	84.4	76.7	2.126	.091
Previously committed aggravated assault	74.6	64.0	2.942	.106
Previously involved in a gang fight	74.7	62.0	4.080*	.126*
Previously used weapon to commit crime	73.5	64.4	1.868	.084
Previously engaged in robbery	75.3	65.5	3.052	.107
Used small caliber gun to commit crime	79.6	66.3	5.173*	.140*
Used medium caliber gun to commit crime	76.6	60.0	7.918*	.173*
Used large caliber gun to commit crime	76.6	67.1	2.821	.103
Used automatic gun to commit crime	83.8	66.5	7.362*	.167*
Used shotgun to commit crime	82.0	67.6	4.671*	.133*
Currently or ever been a gang member	75.8	60.9	6.313*	.154*
Previously sold marijuana	74.1	51.4	8.008*	.174*
Previously sold drugs other than marijuana	76.4	60.4	7.418*	.167*
Previously used marijuana	72.9	61.4	2.349	.094
Previously used drugs other than marijuana	73.3	66.7	1.271	.069

* $p < .05$

CHAPTER 4
What Guns Do Juveniles Prefer?

In the previous chapter, we reviewed the sources of gun acquisition among the youths in this sample. We determined that the youths prefer to obtain guns by purchasing them on the streets, borrowing or stealing them from relatives, or stealing them from a number of other sources. In this chapter, we begin by summarizing the extant literature regarding which guns juveniles prefer to carry then return to the responses surrounding that issue from our sample.

Review of Previous Work on Gun Preferences

Sheley and Wright (1995) determined that 83% of the inmate sample owned a firearm at the time they were incarcerated. Among these youths, the most commonly owned firearm was a revolver (72% had owned one at one point in their life, and 58% owned a revolver at the time of their incarceration). Two-thirds of the sample had owned automatic and semiautomatic handguns at some point, with 55% owning an automatic or semiautomatic handgun at the time of their incarceration. About half of the youth owned a sawed-off shotgun, and 39% owned a regular shotgun at the time of their incarceration. Finally, about one-third of the incarcerated boys owned an assault weapon (i.e., military-style automatic or semiautomatic rifle) at the time of their incarceration.

In the Wright and Rossi (1986) study, three in four respondents admitted that they owned firearms. As the authors suggest, though, this is probably a conservative estimate, as a number of respondents who admitted to being armed when they committed a crime denied that they owned guns. Of those that had owned a gun, the vast majority (87%) owned a handgun, the firearm most regularly used in firearm-related crimes (Federal Bureau of Investigation 2003). Despite a large proportion of handgun owners in the sample, few owned the guns legally (85% had never applied for a permit to purchase or carry their handgun). A full 50% reported having fired a gun at somebody else. Wright and Rossi (1986) then turned to those respondents who were actually armed during the crime for which they went to prison (54% of their sample). Of this number, 60% were armed with a handgun, 15% were armed with a sawed-off shotgun or rifle, and 11% were armed with a regular shoulder weapon. Finally, about one in three (30%) of the respondents carried a weapon "more or less all the time."

What Guns Do Respondents in this Sample Prefer?

Youths in this study were asked to identify the types of guns that they used in the commission of a crime. The respondents were asked to list all of the kinds of guns that they used to commit crimes with. We took the total list and created seven categories. Guns were categorized as being small caliber handguns, medium caliber handguns, large caliber handguns, automatic (including semi-automatic) guns, shotguns, rifles, and other types of firearms. A list of the specific guns that were classified into each category is provided in table 4.1.

Date on the prevalence of each type of gun being used in the commission of a crime is presented in table 4.2. In this sample, 13.4% reported using a small caliber handgun to commit crimes in the past. Twenty-four percent of the sample reported using a medium caliber handgun to commit crimes. Almost 15% of the sample claimed to use a large caliber handgun to commit crimes. Almost 9% of the sample reported using an automatic or semi-automatic weapon to commit a crime in the past. A similar proportion reported using a shotgun in the commission of a crime. Fewer than 2% of the sample reported using a rifle to commit crimes. As such, we do not consider rifles further in the analysis reported below.

The youths in this sample were not as actively involved in using guns to commit crimes as Sheley and Wright (1995) found in their sample of incarcerated juvenile males. In their study, they found that 83% had at some point possessed a gun. In our sample, we found that 47% reported ever owning a gun. In addition, 36.2% of this sample reported having bought a gun at some point. Sheley and Wright found 40% of their sample to have procured a gun specifically for criminal activities. In our sample, 32% reported using a gun to commit crimes in the past. The lower prevalence of using guns to commit crimes makes sense in the context of our sample. We include females in our sample, and we have included youths from all state-run correctional facilities. This means we have youths in the sample who were not classified to the maximum-security facilities.

In trying to further understand the choices that juvenile offenders make in selecting a weapon to use in the commission of a crime, we find that the actual type of gun does not seem to be a significant choice for these youths. The differences in selection of gun type across categories of criminal activity, gang membership, carrying guns for protection, and demographic characteristics are considered in tables 4.3-4.7. Each table considers one of the five gun types we examine here: small-caliber handguns, medium-caliber handguns, large-caliber handguns, shotguns, and automatic or semi-automatic gun.

In brief, we find few factors that help us to clarify why the youths would select one type of gun over another. Across the five tables we find similar patterns. Race, public assistance, and previous victimization experiences do not help clarify the choice for a particular type of gun. Every other variable we consider, though, is significantly related to the choice of gun, regardless of the type of gun.

In this sample, 13% of the youths reported using a small caliber handgun to commit a crime. Several factors increase the prevalence of using a small caliber handgun. Among those youths who have committed a robbery in the past, 30% have used a small caliber handgun to commit crimes. Among those youths who carried a gun for protection, 28% reported using a small caliber handgun in the commission of a crime. In the group of youths who have at one time been a gang member, 26% reported using small caliber handguns to commit crimes. Similar prevalence rates are reported for those youths who have sold drugs other than marijuana and those who have been in a gang fight in the past.

These same factors are associated with higher prevalence rates of using the other four types of guns. When we consider the prevalence for each gun type in the total sample, each of these variables is associated with doubling that rate. For instance, in the full sample, 24% reported using medium caliber handguns to commit a crime. That rate increases to 43% for those who have been in a gang fight and for those who have sold drugs other than marijuana. Among those who have been members of a gang, 47% have used medium caliber handguns in the commission of a crime. Even higher rates are found among those who have committed robberies (48%) and among those carrying gun for protection (50%).

In the full sample, 15% of the respondents report using a large caliber handgun to commit a crime. This rate is significantly higher for those who sold drugs other than marijuana (26%), those who have been involved in a gang fight (27%), those reporting having been a gang member (28%), those who have committed robberies in the past (28%), and those who carried a gun for protection (31%). The prevalence of using an automatic or semi-automatic weapon in the commission of a crime is 9% in the full sample. This rate is significantly higher for those who sold drugs other than marijuana (18%), those who have been involved in a gang fight (16%), those reporting having been a gang member (17%), those who have committed robberies in the past (17%), and those who carried a gun for protection (19%). Finally, the prevalence of using a shotgun in the commission of a crime is 9% in the full sample. This rate is significantly higher for those who sold drugs other than marijuana (15%), those who have been involved in a gang fight (15%), those reporting having been a gang member (14%), those who have committed robberies in the past (15%), and those who carried a gun for protection (18%).

When we look only at the subsample of youths who have used a gun to commit a crime in the past, we are able to detect some differences. Tables 4.7-4.11 present results from these analyses. We find that among those youths who have used a gun to commit crimes in the past, those who have sold marijuana are more likely to have used a medium-caliber handgun to commit crimes than those who haven't sold marijuana. Those who sold drugs other than marijuana were more likely to have used a small-caliber handgun in the commission of a crime. Those youths who have been gang members at some point in the past were more likely to have used a small-caliber or medium-caliber handgun in the commission of a crime. Selling drugs and membership in a gang, however, are not related to a higher likelihood of using any other type of gun to commit a crime. Those who have committed robberies in the past are more likely to have used small-caliber handguns in their criminal activities. Finally, males are more likely to have used large-caliber handguns than females among those youths who have used guns to commit crimes.

Qualitative Results

From the life-history narrative data that we have available, we can examine the different types of guns that these youths have access to, that they "own" and that they are using when they commit crimes. The youths were asked open-ended questions about the kinds of guns they had access to. For instance, Ed tells us:

> *Have you ever owned a gun?*
> Yes.
> *What kind?*
> I don't know.
> *You don't know?*
> A lot.
> *A lot? What kind?*
> A .22, a 9, I had a 12 gauge, I had a .38 a .45 an AR-15...

Michael, another youth in the life-history study, provides the following information on guns that he owned:

> *Were there any guns that you owned?*
> A 12 gauge, .38....
> *How did you get those guns?*
> Just around you know, people....
> *They just give them to you?*
> I bought them.

Another youth, Casper, describes the gun that he carried:

> I started selling drugs at school. I carried marijuana in school. I carried a 12 gauge to school. I was smoking weed inside the classroom. I was arrested because I tried to sell guns.

At another point in the interview, Casper noted

> My first gun was a .25, it was little.

When asked about the number of guns that he had in total, Casper responded

I had a .22 rifle, a .12-gauge and a .25. That was it.

Another youth, Guy, talks about the different kinds of guns he and his friends had access to.

> They pull out their guns, we pull our guns, they had little .25's and stuff like that we had tech 9's, Uzi's, .40 cals, .50 cals, we had all that.

Corey, when asked what kinds of guns he had owned, noted

> *Have you ever owned a gun?*
> Yeah.
> *What kind?*
> Just about every kind of gun there is but, you know, I ain't never had a MAC 11 or a MAC 10. I owned a .38 special, .38 super, Glock 9, Glock .45, .40 caliber, .44 caliber, .50 caliber.

Another youth, Grant, listed the guns he had in his possession previously:

> *Have you ever owned a gun?*
> Yeah. I've had a few guns.
> *What kind of guns?*
> .380, 9 millimeter, .25's. I had, we stole a AK-47 assault rifle one time.

Still another youth, Ignis, talked about one gun he owned and others that he carried:

> *Have you ever owned a gun?*
> Yes I have.
> *What kind of gun?*
> A .45 Magnum.
> *How did you get it?*
> My stepdad.
> *Was it his gun or your gun?*
> It's more my gun, I have a permit, but it's more of a forged permit.
> *How did you do that?*
> He was an ex-owner of a gun shop.
> *So he got you this gun illegally?*
> Well, kind of.
> *Was that the first time you ever had a gun?*
> No, before that I was always carrying around .45s.

Edmundo, another youth, describes two guns he stole from his father:

> I was like 13 or 14 years old and had a .38 special, then I had a .380.

Some youths used guns at times, even when they did not own or carry them on their person. Fred provides one example:

> *Have you ever owned a gun?*
> No.
> *So you've never used a gun before?*
> Well, I shot a 22 shotgun before and a 25.
> *How did you have access to those guns?*
> My friends.

J.R. provides another example of the kind of gun that the youths were able to get from their friends and family:

> *Have you ever owned a gun?*
> Yep.
> *How did you get it?*
> I got it from my cousin and she got it from a dude that use to be up here. I took it from my cousin
> *You took it from him?*
> Yes.
> *You stole it from him?*
> No, I took it. I was like give it to me and I didn't give it back to him.
> *What kind of a gun was it?*
> It was a .380.
> *So how long did you have it for?*
> About three weeks.
> *Did you use it for anything?*
> Nope.
> *Just carried it around?*
> Yeah all the time.

Tables

TABLE 4.1 Firearms categorized by type

Small-Caliber Handgun	Medium-Caliber Handgun	Large-Caliber Handgun	Automatic or Semi-Automatic	Shotgun
.22	.32	.40 cal	AK	Shotgun
.22 cal	.32 revolver	Glock .40	AK-45	12 gauge
.22 handgun	Glock model .32	.44	AK-47	12 pump
.22 revolver	.357	Smith and	AR15	20 gauge
.22 Berretta	.357 Magnum	Wesson .44	Mac 10	Remington pump
Ruger .22	.357 Special	.45	Uzi	Mossberg
Taurus .22	.357 Stubnose	.45 cal	Tek 9	Sawed-off
Tek .22	.38	.45 Gooseneck	Automatic rifle	shotgun
Dillenger	.38 cal	Ruger .45	Automatic shot-	Pump
.25	.38 Special	.45 SK	gun	Riot pump
.25 cal	.38 Snub nose	Colt .45		
.25 pistol	.38 revolver	.50 cal		
Titan .25	.380	Grizzly .50 cal		
	Baby .380			
	9			
	9mm			
	Glock 9			
	M9			

TABLE 4.2 Gun type youths committed crimes with

Type of Gun	Full Sample (% yes)	Gun Criminals (% yes)
Small-caliber handgun	13.4	35.1
Medium-caliber handgun	24.0	66.0
Large-caliber handgun	14.6	40.4
Automatic or semi-automatic firearm	8.8	25.7
Shotgun	8.9	23.0
Rifle	1.6	4.2
Other type of gun	6.3	13.6

TABLE 4.3 Analysis of whether respondent has used a small-caliber handgun to commit a crime

Predictor	Yes (%)	No (%)	χ^2	Phi
Female	5.4	15.4	11.401*	-.117*
Nonwhite	15.4	11.4	2.867	.059
Family received public assistance	13.9	13.9	.001	-.001
Experienced personal victimization	14.5	11.3	1.166	.038
Carried a gun for protection	28.3	3.8	97.314*	.349*
Previously committed simple assault	18.7	6.3	22.162*	.169*
Previously committed aggravated assault	22.7	8.0	33.638*	.208*
Previously involved in a gang fight	25.5	5.8	60.549*	.279*
Previously used weapon to commit crime	23.9	5.8	55.269*	.260*
Previously engaged in robbery	30.0	6.8	78.363*	.308*
Currently or ever been a gang member	26.4	6.0	68.296*	.287*
Previously sold marijuana	19.1	5.9	30.886*	.193*
Previously sold drugs other than marijuana	26.0	6.1	65.497*	.281*
Previously used marijuana	15.3	8.9	6.137*	.086*
Previously used drugs other than marijuana	17.6	9.6	11.480*	.118*

* p<.05

TABLE 4.4 Analysis of whether respondent has used a medium-caliber handgun to commit a crime

Predictor	Yes (%)	No (%)	χ^2	Phi
Female	9.6	27.6	23.565*	-.169*
Nonwhite	25.8	22.5	1.186	.038
Family received public assistance	27.3	24.7	.606	.028
Experienced personal victimization	25.6	22.6	.647	.028
Carried a gun for protection	50.2	7.6	186.260*	.483*
Previously committed simple assault	31.7	13.6	30.700*	.199*
Previously committed aggravated assault	40.6	13.9	71.699*	.304*
Previously involved in a gang fight	42.9	11.9	97.134*	.354*
Previously used weapon to commit crime	42.9	10.2	116.590*	.378*
Previously engaged in robbery	47.7	14.6	101.682*	.350*
Currently or ever been a gang member	47.2	11.0	137.058*	.407*
Previously sold marijuana	36.6	7.5	93.954*	.337*
Previously sold drugs other than marijuana	43.1	13.0	95.565*	.340*
Previously used marijuana	29.3	11.7	29.135*	.188*
Previously used drugs other than marijuana	33.0	16.0	32.565*	.198*

* p<.05

TABLE 4.5 Analysis of whether respondent has used a large-caliber handgun to commit a crime

Predictor	Yes (%)	No (%)	χ^2	Phi
Female	3.0	17.5	22.396*	-.164*
Nonwhite	16.6	12.6	2.623	.057
Family received public assistance	16.3	15.3	.122	.013
Experienced personal victimization	15.9	12.4	1.304	.040
Carried a gun for protection	30.5	4.7	99.761*	.354*
Previously committed simple assault	19.4	8.5	16.208*	.145*
Previously committed aggravated assault	24.8	8.6	37.604*	.220*
Previously involved in a gang fight	27.1	6.9	58.666*	.275*
Previously used weapon to commit crime	26.4	5.8	67.512*	.288*
Previously engaged in robbery	27.8	9.3	46.609*	.237*
Currently or ever been a gang member	28.1	7.0	68.154*	.287*
Previously sold marijuana	21.3	5.9	38.677*	.216*
Previously sold drugs other than marijuana	25.7	8.2	46.958*	.238*
Previously used marijuana	18.2	6.1	20.577*	.158*
Previously used drugs other than marijuana	19.9	9.8	16.901*	.143*

* p<.05

TABLE 4.6 Analysis of whether respondent has used an automatic or semi-automatic gun to commit a crime

Predictor	Yes (%)	No (%)	χ^2	Phi
Female	2.4	10.4	10.601*	-.113*
Nonwhite	10.4	7.4	2.173	.052
Family received public assistance	9.8	9.2	.078	.010
Experienced personal victimization	9.0	9.6	.060	-.009
Carried a gun for protection	19.1	2.3	65.041*	.285*
Previously committed simple assault	10.5	6.6	3.230	.065
Previously committed aggravated assault	13.4	5.9	12.937*	.129*
Previously involved in a gang fight	16.1	3.8	34.972*	.212*
Previously used weapon to commit crime	16.2	3.5	39.785*	.221*
Previously engaged in robbery	16.9	5.6	26.840*	.180*
Currently or ever been a gang member	17.4	4.0	42.805*	.227*
Previously sold marijuana	13.4	2.8	28.461*	.185*
Previously sold drugs other than marijuana	17.8	3.6	47.829*	.240*
Previously used marijuana	10.3	5.3	5.528*	.082*
Previously used drugs other than marijuana	12.0	5.9	9.460*	.107*

* p<.05

TABLE 4.7 Analysis of whether respondent has used a shotgun to commit a crime

Predictor	Yes (%)	No (%)	χ^2	Phi
Female	4.2	10.1	5.684*	-.083*
Nonwhite	8.7	9.4	.133	-.013
Family received public assistance	10.6	8.8	.662	.030
Experienced personal victimization	10.1	6.2	2.512	.056
Carried a gun for protection	17.5	3.6	44.522*	.236*
Previously committed simple assault	11.5	5.5	7.446*	.098*
Previously committed aggravated assault	14.9	5.2	20.966*	.164*
Previously involved in a gang fight	15.2	5.1	22.470*	.170*
Previously used weapon to commit crime	15.1	4.5	26.814*	.181*
Previously engaged in robbery	14.8	6.6	13.871*	.129*
Currently or ever been a gang member	14.4	5.9	17.043*	.143*
Previously sold marijuana	13.4	3.1	26.653*	.179*
Previously sold drugs other than marijuana	14.8	5.5	20.306*	.157*
Previously used marijuana	10.5	5.3	5.838*	.084*
Previously used drugs other than marijuana	13.6	4.8	19.411*	.153*

* $p<.05$

TABLE 4.8 Analysis of whether gun criminals have used a small-caliber handgun to commit a crime

Predictor	Yes (%)	No (%)	χ^2	Phi
Female	24.0	36.3	1.492	-.075
Nonwhite	35.9	33.6	.150	.024
Family received public assistance	36.8	34.9	.085	.019
Experienced personal victimization	35.5	33.3	.082	.018
Carried a gun for protection	37.5	25.9	2.521	.098
Previously committed simple assault	38.0	26.1	2.344	.095
Previously committed aggravated assault	35.7	36.0	.002	.003
Previously involved in a gang fight	39.2	28.2	2.731	.103
Previously used weapon to commit crime	36.8	30.5	.784	.055
Previously engaged in robbery	43.8	24.4	10.906*	.203*
Currently or ever been a gang member	39.9	25.3	5.469*	.144*
Previously sold marijuana	35.1	35.1	.000	.000
Previously sold drugs other than marijuana	40.8	24.2	7.253*	.165*
Previously used marijuana	34.8	36.4	.037	-.012
Previously used drugs other than marijuana	35.5	34.4	.030	.011

* $p<.05$

TABLE 4.9 Analysis of whether gun criminals have used a medium-caliber handgun to commit a crime

Predictor	Yes (%)	No (%)	χ^2	Phi
Female	52.0	67.5	2.425	-.096
Nonwhite	62.1	71.8	2.704	-.101
Family received public assistance	77.6	64.5	4.197*	.131*
Experienced personal victimization	67.3	64.6	.129	.022
Carried a gun for protection	69.2	57.4	2.702	.102
Previously committed simple assault	68.1	60.9	.886	.058
Previously committed aggravated assault	67.6	64.0	.305	.034
Previously involved in a gang fight	69.4	59.2	2.401	.097
Previously used weapon to commit crime	69.1	55.9	3.554	.116
Previously engaged in robbery	70.5	60.5	2.949	.105
Currently or ever been a gang member	73.6	50.6	13.808*	.228*
Previously sold marijuana	68.4	51.4	4.136*	.125*
Previously sold drugs other than marijuana	69.0	60.4	1.937	.085
Previously used marijuana	67.4	59.1	1.135	.065
Previously used drugs other than marijuana	68.0	62.4	.861	.057

* p<.05

TABLE 4.10 Analysis of whether gun criminals have used a large-caliber handgun to commit a crime

Predictor	Yes (%)	No (%)	χ^2	Phi
Female	16.0	42.9	6.814*	-.160*
Nonwhite	39.2	41.8	.180	-.026
Family received public assistance	48.7	39.6	1.753	.085
Experienced personal victimization	41.1	39.6	.038	.012
Carried a gun for protection	42.3	35.2	.900	.059
Previously committed aggravated assault	41.1	41.3	.001	.002
Previously committed simple assault	41.8	39.1	.110	.021
Previously involved in a gang fight	44.6	32.4	3.171	.111
Previously used weapon to commit crime	42.2	33.9	1.297	.070
Previously engaged in robbery	40.4	40.3	.000	.001
Currently or ever been a gang member	43.8	33.3	2.670	.100
Previously sold marijuana	40.8	37.8	.115	.021
Previously sold drugs other than marijuana	40.8	39.6	.038	.012
Previously used marijuana	42.5	29.5	2.571	.099
Previously used drugs other than marijuana	40.1	40.9	.014	-.007

* p<.05

TABLE 4.11 Analysis of whether gun criminals have used an automatic or semi-automatic gun to commit a crime

Predictor	Yes (%)	No (%)	χ^2	Phi
Female	16.0	26.7	1.350	-.071
Nonwhite	25.5	26.4	.025	-.010
Family received public assistance	28.9	26.0	.226	.030
Experienced personal victimization	24.8	31.3	.858	-.057
Carried a gun for protection	27.9	18.5	1.957	.086
Previously committed simple assault	23.9	32.6	1.496	-.076
Previously committed aggravated assault	22.7	32.0	2.435	-.097
Previously involved in a gang fight	26.3	22.5	.395	.039
Previously used weapon to commit crime	27.5	20.3	1.207	.068
Previously engaged in robbery	25.3	26.1	.017	-.008
Currently or ever been a gang member	27.5	21.8	.991	.061
Previously sold marijuana	25.9	24.3	.040	.012
Previously sold drugs other than marijuana	28.7	19.8	2.512	.097
Previously used marijuana	25.3	27.3	.072	-.016
Previously used drugs other than marijuana	25.6	25.8	.002	-.002

TABLE 4.12 Analysis of whether gun criminals have used a shotgun to commit a crime

Predictor	Yes (%)	No (%)	χ^2	Phi
Female	28.0	22.5	.387	.038
Nonwhite	20.9	26.4	1.066	-.064
Family received public assistance	25.0	23.1	.107	.021
Experienced personal victimization	23.8	20.8	.197	.027
Carried a gun for protection	23.1	24.1	.024	-.010
Previously committed simple assault	22.1	28.3	.816	-.056
Previously committed aggravated assault	23.2	22.7	.010	.006
Previously involved in a gang fight	23.1	25.4	.142	-.023
Previously used weapon to commit crime	23.0	23.7	.012	-.007
Previously engaged in robbery	20.5	26.1	1.120	-.065
Currently or ever been a gang member	21.3	26.4	.854	-.057
Previously sold marijuana	24.1	16.2	1.123	.065
Previously sold drugs other than marijuana	22.4	24.2	.105	-.020
Previously used marijuana	23.1	22.7	.003	.003
Previously used drugs other than marijuana	25.6	18.3	1.816	.083

CHAPTER 5

Why Do Juvenile Gun Criminals Choose the Guns They Use?

What the Research Tells Us

As suggested throughout this book, firearms are a prevalent part of the criminal offender's lifestyle. Some research suggests that firearms are necessary "tools" that many criminals use to conduct their criminal business (Sheley & Wright 1995). Wright and Rossi (1986) suggest that individuals engaging in gun crimes often choose to arm themselves for protection from potentially aggressive victims. A number of researchers have suggested that firearms make victims less likely to resist offenders, less likely to be harmed in criminal transactions such as robbery, and more likely to make a successful completion of a criminal offense for the offender (Zimring and Hawkins 1997).

Birkbeck et al. (1999) asked their sample of incarcerated adolescents both why kids (not necessarily themselves) used guns and why they personally used guns. The respondents in their sample suggested that the primary motivations for firearm use were protection and revenge, both among kids in general (33.5% for protection and 22.0% "to get revenge") and in their own personal choices (31.8% for protection and 32.6% to get revenge). Thus, both protection and revenge are important motivations for gun "use" among their sample.

The most definitive work regarding the motivations for choice of firearms among adolescents is once again the work of Sheley and Wright (1995). Sheley and Wright asked two questions that (at least tangentially) measure motivations for firearm choice among juvenile offenders. First, almost half (45%) of the youth in their sample felt that using a weapon in crime decreased the chance that a victim would resist the offender and a slightly smaller percentage (42%) agreed that people do not want to "mess with" an offender who uses a weapon (62). Furthermore, four in five respondents (80%) in their sample felt that a very important reason for carrying a weapon during crime was so that an offender could be ready to defend himself against an a potential victim, while almost three in five (58%) respondents expressed concern that a victim might be armed.

Almost half of the respondents agreed that other "very important" reasons for arming oneself when engaging in crime were that: an offender might need a weapon to escape (49%); a victim would be less likely to resist an armed offender (45%); and people don't "mess with" an armed offender (42%) (Sheley & Wright 1995, 62).

Additionally, Sheley and Wright (1995) queried their respondents who had obtained a firearm to rate the "importance" of a variety of reasons regarding why they obtained their "most recent" firearm (73). For each type of firearm in question (military-style guns, handguns, and rifles or shotguns), at least three in five respondents (73% for military-style guns, 74% for handguns, and 64% for rifles or shotguns) stated that protection was a very important reason for obtaining their most recent firearm. Thus, regardless of the type of firearm used by delinquent youth, one of the most important reasons that adolescent offenders arm themselves is for protection against victims.

Sheley and Wright (1995) were also able to examine the impact of whether a youth sold or used drugs on the type of firearm they normally carried. Their findings suggest that those who use drugs and those who sell drugs were more likely to possess each type of firearm in question (e.g., revolvers, automatic or semiautomatic handguns, military style automatic or semi-automatic rifles, regular shotguns, and sawed-off shotguns). Additionally, heavy users who sold drugs were significantly more likely to possess automatic or semiautomatic handguns and military-style automatic and semiautomatic rifles than those who participated in 'heavy" drug use but did not sell drugs as were those who sold but did not use drugs. Consequently, the public perception that youth who sell drugs are armed appears to be an accurate perception; the perception that they are often armed with automatic or semiautomatic handguns or rifles has some support as well (Sheley & Wright 1995).

Sheley and Wright (1995) considered the possibility that the youths in their sample carried guns to earn the respect of others. They asked the respondents to indicate their degree of agreement with the statements "In my crowd, if you don't have a gun people don't respect you," and "My friends would look down on me if I did not carry a gun." Incarcerated youths in their sample showed little agreement with these statements as the motivation for their own gun carrying. Even when they focused only on those youths who carry guns, they found over fifty percent of the respondents to disagree with these statements.

Assessing the Reason for Carrying Guns

For our survey, we asked the youths to express how important the following reasons were in influencing the decision to carry a gun or other weapon. The youths were to indicate whether the reasons were "very important", "somewhat important", or "not important." The potential reasons included:

- If I am planning a crime, there is always a chance a victim might be armed
- You have to be ready to defend yourself

- If you have a weapon when you commit a crime, your victim doesn't put up a fight and you don't have to hurt them
- I feel I might need a weapon to escape from a situation
- People just don't mess with you when you have a weapon
- In my crowd, if you don't have a gun, people don't respect you
- My friends would look down on me if I didn't carry a gun

The results of our analysis are strikingly similar to the results from the Sheley and Wright study. In table 5.1, we present the percentage in the total sample and among those who have used guns to commit crimes in the past that indicate that each of these reasons is either very important or somewhat important. In the full sample, 74% indicated that the potential need to defend against an armed victim was an important reason to carry a gun. Eighty-four percent of the sample thought it was important to carry a gun so that you were prepared to defend yourself. Almost three-fourths of the sample (72%) thought that it was important to have a weapon so the victim does not put up a fight and there is not a reason to hurt the victim. Consistent with this theme of self-defense, 62% thought an important reason to carry a gun was so to allow for a means to escape from a situation and 61% felt it was important to carry a gun so that people did not "mess" with you. In contrast, less than one-quarter (23%) of the sample thought it would be important to carry a gun to earn people's respect. A similarly small proportion of the sample (22%) reported that it was important to carry a gun because your friends would look down on you if you failed to do so. The priority for protection and lack of importance related to respect mirrored the results from the Sheley and Wright sample.

When we look just at the youths who have committed crimes in the past with guns, we find even stronger support for the belief that one should carry guns for protection. The patterns are similar, but this group reports more agreement that each of these statements is an important reason to carry a gun. The two items that tap into respect and others' view of them are still not seen as very important reasons for carrying guns.

We also consider whether attitudes about the reasons to carry guns are influenced by the previous involvement of the youths in violence, victimization, drugs and gang activity. We examine differences across demographic categories. These results are reported below separately for the full sample and for the sub-sample of gun criminals in tables 5.2-5.15. Here we find that the previous involvement of the youths in violent, drug, and gang activity enhances the perception that it is important to carry a gun for protection and to be prepared against potential danger.

In table 5.2, we examine the attitude that it is important to carry a gun because "If I am planning a crime, there is always a chance a victim might be armed." In the full sample, 74% of the youths felt this was an important reason for carrying a gun. The percentage feeling this way increases significantly among those youths who have carried a gun for protection (89% rate this reason as important), those who have previously engaged in robbery (88%), those who previously sold drugs other than marijuana (88%), and those who previously used a weapon to commit a crime (86%). Beyond these associations, we find that every criminal activity we consider, with the exception of the use of marijuana, is has a statistically significant relationship with the likelihood of rating the "chance a victim might be armed" as an important reason for carrying a gun. Males are more likely than females to rate this reason as important, and nonwhites are significantly more likely than whites to rate this as important. We find no differences based on the receipt of public assistance or having been the victim of a violent crime in the past.

We repeat the analysis from table 5.2 in table 5.3 for the subsample of youths who have previously committed a crime with a gun. Having had the experience of committing a crime with a gun before, the vast majority of the youths (over 92%) agree that it is important to carry a gun because a victim might be armed. There are very few experiences or factors that help to further differentiate which gun criminals are most likely to express this view. The only significant differences found in table 6.3 are for those gun criminals who have previously sold drugs (both marijuana and other drugs as well).

In tables 5.4 and 5.5, we examine the attitude that it is important to carry a gun because "You have to be ready to defend yourself." In the full sample, this was the statement that received the greatest agreement that it was an important reason to carry a gun. For the full sample, 84% rated this as an important reason. This percentage reached more than 90% for those youths who carried a gun for protection, had been involved in a gang fight, or had previously engaged in robbery. In addition, there are significant differences found when distinguishing between the youths on all the measures of previous violent offending, gang membership, and drug dealing. We also find that nonwhites are more likely than whites to agree it is important to carry a gun to be ready to defend yourself. In the subsample of gun criminals, we find virtually everyone in the sample (over 90% in each category) agree to the importance of this reason. There are only three instances where this percentage drops below 90%. Those youths who have not used marijuana and those who have not committed an assault against someone else (either simple or aggravated) have the lowest levels of agreement. Only one of these factors (simple assault) is associated with a significant difference on this dimension.

In tables 5.6 and 5.7, we examine predictors of the attitude that it is important to carry a gun because "If you have a weapon when you commit a crime, your victim doesn't put up a fight and you don't have to hurt them." In the full sample, 72% rated this as an important reason to carry a gun. The percentage rating reached over 80% for those who carried a gun for protection, had been in a gang fight, used a weapon to commit a crime, engaged in robbery, had been a gang member, or had sold drugs other than marijuana. Significant differences are found on every dimension we consider, with the exception of public assistance and previous personal victimization experiences. When we consider only those youths who have previously committed a crime with a gun, we find only three factors that significantly differentiate between youths on this attitude.

Among the gun criminals, there are significant differences in the percentage indicating it was important to carry a gun to keep a potential victim from putting up a fight for those youths who have carried a gun for protection, been in a gang fight, or sold drugs other than marijuana.

In tables 5.8 and 5.9, we examine the attitude that it is important to carry a gun because "I feel I might need a weapon to escape from a situation." In the full sample, only 62% indicated it was important to carry a gun for this reason. This level increases to over 75% for those youths who have sold drugs other than marijuana (78%), carried a gun for protection (80%), and engaged in robbery (82%). Again, as above, we find statistically significant differences for each of the measures of previous criminal involvement, with the exception of using drugs. There are also not significant differences based on race or family receipt of public assistance. We find that those who have been the victim of some form of violence are more likely to feel like it would be important to carry a gun to have the ability to escape from a situation. When we consider only those youths who have used a gun to commit a crime, we find significant differences on this attitude for those who have engaged in robbery and those who have sold drugs other than marijuana.

In tables 5.10 and 5.11, we examine the attitude that it is important to carry a gun because "People just don't mess with you when you have a weapon." In the full sample, 61% rated this as an important reason to carry a gun. The strongest differences are found for those youths who have carried a gun for protection, used a weapon to commit a crime, engaged in robbery, joined a gang, or sold drugs other than marijuana. When we restrict our analysis to only the gun criminals, those who sold drugs other than marijuana are significantly more likely to indicate it would be important to carry a gun to keep people from messing with them. There are no other significant differences among the gun criminals on this dimension.

In tables 5.12 and 5.13, we examine the attitude that it is important to carry a gun because "In my crowd, if you don't have a gun, people don't respect you." In the full sample, only 23% rated this an important reason to carry a gun. Among those who had previously engaged in robbery, that percentage increased to 35%. As before, higher percentages in the rating of importance were found also for those youths who previously carried a gun for protection, used a weapon to commit a crime, took part in a gang fight, joined a gang, committed aggravated assault, or sold drugs other than marijuana. Those youths who used marijuana were much less likely to classify this statement as an important reason to carry a gun. When we restricted our assessment to only those youths who have already committed a crime with a gun, only two significant differences remained. Those previously involved in a gang fight were significantly more likely to rate this statement as an important reason for carrying a gun. Also, those who have used marijuana are significantly less likely to rate this statement as an important reason to carrying a firearm.

Finally, in tables 5.14 and 5.15, we examine the attitude that it is important to carry a gun because "My friends would look down on me if I did not carry a gun." As with the item just considered, a very small percentage (22%) of the full sample rated this statement as an important reason to carry a gun. The percentage rating this item as important was even higher for those youths who previously engaged in robbery, carried a gun for protection, used a weapon to commit a crime, or took part in a gang fight. Youths were less likely to rate this item as important if they previously used marijuana. When we restricted the sample to just those offenders who previously used a gun to commit a crime, we find no significant differences in the rating of this item as an important reason for carrying a gun.

To summarize, those youths who have previously committed robberies have the strongest prevalence rates of rating the importance of the protective reasons for carrying a gun. The youths who have sold drugs other than marijuana also have stronger beliefs about the importance of carrying a gun for protection. Other criminal activities that are related with higher rates of protective reasons for carrying guns include gang fights and aggravated assault. In addition, those youths who have been gang members also report stronger attitudes about the protective reasons for carrying guns. In general, having been a victim of violence is not related to these attitudes pertaining to the carrying of guns. It would appear that the perception of risk (i.e., the need to take protective action) is not necessarily related to having experienced violence first hand in the past.

Qualitative Results

From the life-history narrative data that we have available, we can examine the reasons why the youths were carrying guns. The youths were asked to discuss the reasons they carried guns and were allowed to tell the story as they wanted. For instance, Casper tells us

> *How many times have you shot at somebody?*
> If somebody tried to kill me, but I would not think do it to do it. I would not
> feel good about it but it would be his life or mine.

Guy, in describing the kinds of offenses that he has committed over his lifetime, notes

> I was 16, possession of an illegal firearm. I got caught with an AK-47.
> *What were you doing with that?*
> I had it for protection.

At another point in the interview, Guy is describing where he kept a number of guns that he came into possession of:

> *And what would you do with these guns?*
> Before my son was born I had a whole room I use to put nails all in the walls to
> hold my guns, I didn't care. I kept them for protection though. I mean if some-
> body ride up and shoot up the neighborhood you go get to—we called it the lit-
> tle dingo van, it's like our drive by van—get into that and put all our artillery in

there. Whoever shot up our house, we went and shot up their house. There were some days I wanted to carry a .40 cal and some days I wanted to carry a 9. It all depends.
And when you were carrying a gun, where would it be on you?
I always carried a gun.
Where did you carry it?
I had holsters. I had like the police, the one that carries two guns in it, I had like four holsters. I had a sack holster, ankle holster, I had all that. I had holsters that carry two clips on each side and one right here I had all that.

Scott speaks to the issue of whether carrying a gun is a way to change the image others have of him:

How did you get that gun?
It was a friend's of mine.
Then why were you carrying it?
Just 'cause I wanted.
Just to be cool?
No, just 'cause I wanted to carry it.
So how did you carry it, where was it?
I just stuck it in my pants right there.
Was it loaded when you were carrying it?
Yeah.
And you didn't use it to commit any crimes with?
I never used no weapon to commit no crime.

Another youth, Grant, speaks to the issue of carrying a gun for protection:

What would you use the guns for?
To rob people, or just in case somebody tried to rob us. Um, just in case some-body'd start shootin' at us or whatever. Just protection, I guess. Somethin' to have.
Did you ever shoot at somebody?
Oh, I shot at, it was, when we were in Ft. Wayne once and I had a problem with some people, that I shot at 'em. But I don't think that I hit anybody or anything.
So as far as you know you've never shot anybody?
No. I don't think I shot anybody.

Yet another youth, Ignis, speaks to the purpose of having a gun for protection:

Before that I was always carrying around 45s.
Why?
That's what I used to protect myself.
From what?
People that would come up and try to jump me. If I wanted something real bad.
Were you ever in a neighborhood where you were at risk of being jumped?

> Yeah. I had to ride to school in the summer on my bike through a neighborhood that was worse than the one that I was in. People would pick up bricks and throw them at cars as the drove by.

Edmundo provides another example of the perceived need for a gun for personal protection:

> I'm still going to have a gun.
> *Why?*
> 'Cause I need one. 'Cause that's how it is, it's not a stereotype thing or anything, I need a gun because there's people out there that don't like me. Like this dude J____ P____, he lives in the same town as me, he came from Hammond, so he's been to the ghetto, the Latin Kings burned his house down and I'm buddies with the Latin Kings. But that's not what made him mad. He's been going with this girl, E_____. She had her baby and they were going to get married, well she cheated on him with me on my sixteenth birthday.

In another part of the interview, Edmundo reflected again on the issue of protection:

> We didn't need to do that, but we did it. I can't change the past, and if I could go back I wouldn't have done it, 'cause I just put myself in stupid situations like that. The guns really helped me 'cause I needed to have protection. But all in all I could have just ran from the guys. I didn't think like that.

Some youths only had experience with guns as part of the time that they spent hanging out with friends. Fred provides an example:

> *How did you have access to those guns?*
> My friends.
> *You were just shooting to be shooting?*
> We were shooting in the river.
> *In the river?*
> In the water, aiming at the water and shooting.

In this next excerpt, Ed provides an example of how having a gun facilitates safer criminal activity:

> *Do you feel safer to have a gun?*
> Yeah to tell you the truth.
> *Powerful?*
> Not powerful but it made me feel like at the time I was selling drugs and I was when I say I was real interested in selling drugs I only say like I was this big drug dealer or nothing but I was real interested in drugs then. It's like when you have a gun you be like well you know there's a chance you can get robbed but you be like you ain't going to worry about it cause he got a gun you got a gun one of you all is going to get shot you know what I mean.

In his interview, Michael describes feeling a need for a gun when he expected there to be potential violence:

> *Did you carry a gun on you a lot?*
> I would like if we was going to go somewhere and I thought there might be a problem or even if we just went somewhere shit you know or like if we go somewhere and like my cousin call me up and say hey man you know these dudes are down here O.K. well I will be down there. I would take it with me

Tables

TABLE 5.1 Reasons to carry a gun

Reason	Full Sample [a]	Gun Criminals [a]
If planning a crime, there is chance that victim is armed	74.3	92.3
To be ready to defend self	84.1	93.1
Victim does not put up fight and does not have to be hurt	71.5	83.3
Might need a weapon to escape a situation	61.5	80.0
People don't mess with you when you have a weapon	61.0	73.5
If don't have gun, people don't respect	23.2	32.4
Friends would look down on if did not carry a gun	22.0	27.8

[a] Percentages in each group indicating very important or somewhat important.

TABLE 5.2 Important to carry gun because "there is always a chance a victim might be armed"

Predictor	Yes (%)	No (%)	χ^2	Phi
Female	60.0	77.9	18.834*	-.165*
Nonwhite	78.5	69.7	6.943*	.101*
Family received public assistance	73.7	74.8	.084	-.011
Experienced personal victimization	75.5	69.1	2.480	.060
Carried a gun for protection	88.5	62.9	58.237*	.291*
Previously committed simple assault	78.1	66.2	11.126*	.127*
Previously committed aggravated assault	83.9	66.0	28.618*	.204*
Previously involved in a gang fight	85.1	65.1	34.920*	.226*
Previously used weapon to commit crime	86.3	64.4	43.160*	.250*
Previously engaged in robbery	87.8	68.0	30.835*	.211*
Currently or ever been a gang member	83.3	68.0	20.607*	.172*
Previously sold marijuana	82.1	61.6	35.915*	.228*
Previously sold drugs other than marijuana	88.2	64.5	49.150*	.266*
Previously used marijuana	75.2	71.7	.841	.035
Previously used drugs other than marijuana	78.6	69.7	7.245*	.102*

* $p < .05$

TABLE 5.3 Important to carry a gun because "there is always a chance a victim might be armed" (subsample committing a crime with a gun)

Predictor	Yes (%)	No (%)	χ^2	Phi
Female	84.0	93.2	2.716	-.102
Nonwhite	92.7	91.7	.097	.019
Family received public assistance	89.3	94.0	1.611	-.082
Experienced ~~al victimization	92.9	89.6	.586	.048
Carried a g	93.2	88.7	1.211	.068
Previously	93.3	89.1	.951	.061
Previously		88.0	2.583	.100
			192	.028
			00	.119
				.083
			5	.048
			2*	.177*
			6*	.157*
			53	.026
			01	-.002

end yourself"

χ^2	Phi
3.533	-.071
4.875*	.084*
.002	-.002
.186	.016
24.648*	.188*
8.573*	.111*
9.406*	.117*
14.930*	.147*
10.140*	.121*
12.980*	.136*
10.647*	.123*
7.084*	.101*
11.847*	.130*
1.677	.049
1.758	.050

* p<.05

TABLE 5.5 Important to carry a gun because "you have to be ready to defend yourself"
(subsample committing a crime with a gun)

Predictor	Yes (%)	No (%)	χ^2	Phi
Female	92.0	93.2	.050	-.014
Nonwhite	92.7	93.5	.070	-.016
Family received public assistance	92.0	93.4	.149	-.025
Experienced personal victimization	92.3	95.8	.729	-.053
Carried a gun for protection	93.2	92.5	.033	.011
Previously committed simple assault	95.2	84.8	6.536*	.160*
Previously committed aggravated assault	95.0	89.3	2.732	.104
Previously involved in a gang fight	93.5	92.6	.055	.015
Previously used weapon to commit crime	93.5	91.5	.275	.033
Previously engaged in robbery	95.1	90.5	2.130	.091
Currently or ever been a gang member	93.2	92.9	.009	.006
Previously sold marijuana	92.9	94.4	.121	-.022
Previously sold drugs other than marijuana	92.4	94.4	.358	-.037
Previously used marijuana	94.4	86.4	3.704	.119
Previously used drugs other than marijuana	92.9	93.4	.024	-.010

* $p<.05$

TABLE 5.6 Important to carry a gun because "if you have a weapon, your victim doesn't
put up a fight and you don't have to hurt them"

Predictor	Yes (%)	No (%)	χ^2	Phi
Female	64.8	73.3	3.989*	-.076*
Nonwhite	75.3	67.8	4.684*	.083*
Family received public assistance	72.3	70.5	.217	.018
Experienced personal victimization	72.8	67.3	1.731	.050
Carried a gun for protection	82.1	63.3	29.225*	.206*
Previously committed simple assault	74.7	64.3	7.944*	.108*
Previously committed aggravated assault	77.4	66.2	10.404*	.123*
Previously involved in a gang fight	82.6	62.3	34.001*	.224*
Previously used weapon to commit crime	80.4	64.4	21.727*	.178*
Previously engaged in robbery	84.1	65.7	24.983*	.190*
Currently or ever been a gang member	82.1	64.1	26.603*	.196*
Previously sold marijuana	77.9	61.3	22.309*	.180*
Previously sold drugs other than marijuana	83.2	63.3	32.685*	.217*
Previously used marijuana	74.1	63.8	6.836*	.099*
Previously used drugs other than marijuana	74.8	68.1	3.844*	.075*

* $p<.05$

TABLE 5.7 Important to carry a gun because "if you have a weapon, your victim doesn't put up a fight and you don't have to hurt them" (subsample committing a crime with a gun)

Predictor	Yes (%)	No (%)	χ^2	Phi
Female	80.0	83.6	.212	-.029
Nonwhite	86.7	79.0	2.606	.101
Family received public assistance	82.4	84.1	.109	-.021
Experienced personal victimization	84.5	81.3	.297	.034
Carried a gun for protection	86.2	73.1	5.187*	.143*
Previously committed simple assault	84.5	75.0	2.327	.096
Previously committed aggravated assault	83.1	82.4	.019	.009
Previously involved in a gang fight	86.7	73.5	6.152*	.157*
Previously used weapon to commit crime	85.4	77.6	1.973	.088
Previously engaged in robbery	86.0	79.8	1.744	.082
Currently or ever been a gang member	85.6	78.3	2.161	.092
Previously sold marijuana	84.7	74.3	2.347	.096
Previously sold drugs other than marijuana	88.3	73.3	9.301*	.190*
Previously used marijuana	85.0	75.0	2.605	.101
Previously used drugs other than marijuana	84.4	81.1	.463	.042

* $p<.05$

TABLE 5.8 Important to carry a gun because "might need a weapon to escape from a situation"

Predictor	Yes (%)	No (%)	χ^2	Phi
Female	45.4	65.6	19.367*	-.167*
Nonwhite	65.6	57.4	4.925*	.084
Family received public assistance	65.6	59.2	2.456	.062
Experienced personal victimization	64.2	52.3	6.950*	.100*
Carried a gun for protection	79.7	47.2	76.603*	.333*
Previously committed simple assault	66.4	50.2	16.924*	.157*
Previously committed aggravated assault	74.1	50.5	40.047*	.241*
Previously involved in a gang fight	73.8	50.5	38.472*	.237*
Previously used weapon to commit crime	74.8	50.5	42.462*	.248*
Previously engaged in robbery	81.5	52.1	55.272*	.282*
Currently or ever been a gang member	73.9	52.8	31.578*	.213*
Previously sold marijuana	67.4	51.9	16.555*	.154*
Previously sold drugs other than marijuana	77.6	50.2	53.333*	.277*
Previously used marijuana	63.8	54.4	4.837*	.083*
Previously used drugs other than marijuana	64.5	58.2	2.944	.065

* $p<.05$

TABLE 5.9 Important to carry a gun because "might need a weapon to escape from a situation" (subsample committing a crime with a gun)

Predictor	Yes (%)	No (%)	χ^2	Phi
Female	80.0	80.0	.000	.000
Nonwhite	80.7	78.7	.150	.024
Family received public assistance	82.7	79.5	.326	.037
Experienced personal victimization	81.8	75.0	1.158	.067
Carried a gun for protection	82.4	71.7	3.063	.109
Previously committed simple assault	81.3	71.7	2.093	.091
Previously committed aggravated assault	80.6	77.3	.339	.036
Previously involved in a gang fight	81.5	76.5	.797	.056
Previously used weapon to commit crime	80.0	79.7	.003	.004
Previously engaged in robbery	85.4	73.3	5.919*	.151*
Currently or ever been a gang member	81.8	76.2	1.126	.066
Previously sold marijuana	80.4	77.8	.129	.022
Previously sold drugs other than marijuana	84.2	71.9	5.535*	.146*
Previously used marijuana	81.9	70.5	3.016	.108
Previously used drugs other than marijuana	79.3	81.3	.152	-.024

* $p<.05$

TABLE 5.10 Important to carry a gun because "people just don't mess with you when you have a weapon"

Predictor	Yes (%)	No (%)	χ^2	Phi
Female	54.5	62.6	3.126	-.067
Nonwhite	65.9	55.7	7.605*	.105*
Family received public assistance	63.1	59.3	.855	.036
Experienced personal victimization	62.0	57.3	1.072	.039
Carried a gun for protection	73.0	51.7	32.724*	.217*
Previously committed simple assault	64.6	53.7	7.567*	.105*
Previously committed aggravated assault	67.4	55.7	9.857*	.120*
Previously involved in a gang fight	68.3	54.4	13.687*	.141*
Previously used weapon to commit crime	71.7	52.0	28.152*	.202*
Previously engaged in robbery	74.8	54.5	26.068*	.193*
Currently or ever been a gang member	71.4	53.7	22.404*	.179*
Previously sold marijuana	65.3	53.9	9.022*	.114*
Previously sold drugs other than marijuana	73.1	52.6	29.849*	.207*
Previously used marijuana	61.6	59.2	.309	.021
Previously used drugs other than marijuana	63.4	58.3	1.903	.052

* $p<.05$

TABLE 5.11 Important to carry a gun because "people just don't mess with you when you have a weapon" (subsample committing a crime with a gun)

Predictor	Yes (%)	No (%)	χ^2	Phi
Female	68.0	74.0	.423	-.040
Nonwhite	75.3	70.4	.789	.055
Family received public assistance	74.7	72.9	.083	.019
Experienced personal victimization	75.1	66.7	1.433	.075
Carried a gun for protection	76.1	64.2	3.097	.110
Previously committed simple assault	74.0	69.6	.384	.039
Previously committed aggravated assault	73.3	73.3	.000	.000
Previously involved in a gang fight	76.6	64.7	3.617	.120
Previously used weapon to commit crime	74.0	71.2	.185	.027
Previously engaged in robbery	77.8	68.1	3.084	.109
Currently or ever been a gang member	76.1	67.9	1.999	.088
Previously sold marijuana	75.0	63.9	1.964	.087
Previously sold drugs other than marijuana	78.4	64.0	6.155*	.154*
Previously used marijuana	75.0	65.9	1.550	.077
Previously used drugs other than marijuana	74.6	71.4	.297	.034

* p<.05

TABLE 5.12 Important to carry a gun because "in my crowd, if you don't have a gun, people don't respect you"

Predictor	Yes (%)	No (%)	χ^2	Phi
Female	12.8	25.9	10.871*	-.126*
Nonwhite	26.5	20.1	3.860*	.075*
Family received public assistance	22.6	22.2	.014	.005
Experienced personal victimization	22.2	25.9	.889	-.036
Carried a gun for protection	28.8	18.5	10.036*	.121*
Previously committed simple assault	22.6	23.6	.080	-.011
Previously committed aggravated assault	27.4	19.2	6.374*	.097*
Previously involved in a gang fight	30.4	16.2	19.384*	.169*
Previously used weapon to commit crime	28.2	19.1	7.909*	.108*
Previously engaged in robbery	34.5	17.9	23.243*	.184*
Currently or ever been a gang member	28.3	19.7	6.860*	.100*
Previously sold marijuana	25.1	20.2	2.124	.056
Previously sold drugs other than marijuana	28.3	19.7	6.860*	.100*
Previously used marijuana	19.8	33.5	13.448*	-.140*
Previously used drugs other than marijuana	26.0	20.2	3.174	.068

* p<.05

TABLE 5.13 Important to carry a gun because "in my crowd, if you don't have a gun, people don't respect you" (subsample committing a crime with a gun)

Predictor	Yes (%)	No (%)	χ^2	Phi
Female	20.0	33.8	1.952	-.087
Nonwhite	32.7	32.7	.000	.000
Family received public assistance	25.3	33.1	1.477	-.078
Experienced personal victimization	31.1	36.2	.453	-.042
Carried a gun for protection	33.3	28.3	.487	.044
Previously committed simple assault	29.5	41.3	2.438	-.098
Previously committed aggravated assault	33.0	28.0	.603	.049
Previously involved in a gang fight	36.6	16.2	9.666*	.196*
Previously used weapon to commit crime	32.0	32.8	.012	-.007
Previously engaged in robbery	36.1	27.8	2.003	.088
Currently or ever been a gang member	34.3	28.6	.846	.057
Previously sold marijuana	31.8	36.1	.258	-.032
Previously sold drugs other than marijuana	35.9	25.8	2.687	.102
Previously used marijuana	28.7	51.2	8.254*	-.179*
Previously used drugs other than marijuana	33.9	29.7	.488	.043

* p<.05

TABLE 5.14 Important to carry a gun because "friends would look down on me if I did not carry a gun"

Predictor	Yes (%)	No (%)	χ^2	Phi
Female	13.6	24.2	7.350*	-.104*
Nonwhite	26.0	17.9	6.370*	.097*
Family received public assistance	22.0	20.7	.145	.015
Experienced personal victimization	21.2	24.0	.532	-.028
Carried a gun for protection	26.5	18.2	6.748*	.100*
Previously committed simple assault	19.4	25.4	3.228	-.069
Previously committed aggravated assault	24.1	19.7	1.939	.053
Previously involved in a gang fight	25.9	17.7	6.731*	.100*
Previously used weapon to commit crime	25.7	19.2	4.181*	.078*
Previously engaged in robbery	30.7	18.0	14.052*	.143*
Currently or ever been a gang member	24.7	20.1	2.032	.054
Previously sold marijuana	21.4	23.2	.305	-.021
Previously sold drugs other than marijuana	25.4	19.7	3.090	.067
Previously used marijuana	18.4	33.1	16.063*	-.153*
Previously used drugs other than marijuana	22.5	21.6	.079	.011

* p<.05

TABLE 5.15 Important to carry a gun because "friends would look down on me if I did not carry a gun" (subsample committing a crime with a gun)

Predictor	Yes (%)	No (%)	χ^2	Phi
Female	16.0	29.1	1.919	-.086
Nonwhite	30.7	23.4	1.665	.081
Family received public assistance	18.9	27.7	2.110	-.094
Experienced personal victimization	25.8	34.0	1.300	-.071
Carried a gun for protection	28.3	25.0	.225	.030
Previously committed simple assault	24.6	34.8	1.990	-.089
Previously committed aggravated assault	26.8	26.7	.001	.002
Previously involved in a gang fight	29.0	20.6	1.776	.084
Previously used weapon to commit crime	26.4	32.8	.916	-.059
Previously engaged in robbery	32.6	21.7	3.785	.121
Currently or ever been a gang member	28.4	26.5	.102	.020
Previously sold marijuana	26.3	37.1	1.760	-.082
Previously sold drugs other than marijuana	30.4	22.7	1.708	.081
Previously used marijuana	25.5	39.5	3.538	-.117
Previously used drugs other than marijuana	26.3	30.4	.494	-.044

* $p<.05$

CHAPTER 6
Gun Possession: Protection or Aggression

In an environment in which many individuals see themselves as having no power or control over the dangers and fears they face, guns provide a means to reduce fear and regain some defense against ever-present threats and enemies. Some young males may decide that the option of defense through gun use is too attractive to pass up, especially when weighed against the social and mortality costs of not having a firearm accessible. (Wilkinson 2003, 23)

Firearm Possession and Use: Protection?

Researchers such as Wilkinson often cite protection as a reason for weapon possession and provide various explanations for this finding (Asmussen 1992; Bergstein et al. 1996; Birkbeck et al. 1999; Blumstein 1995; Hemenway et al. 1996; May 1999, 2001a; Sheley 1994; Sheley and Brewer 1995; Sheley and Wright 1993; Simon, Dent, and Sussman 1997). In fact, Sheley and Wright (1995) determined that 89% of the gun carriers in their sample of youths in correctional facilities and inner city youths felt that self-protection was a *very important* reason for owning a handgun. Furthermore, the excerpts presented in the previous chapter provide qualitative support for this idea as well.

There have been many studies that have attempted to determine characteristics of adult firearms owners and the motivations for their firearm ownership. One explanation that has surfaced to account for why adults own firearms is the "fear and loathing hypothesis" (Wright, Rossi, and Daly 1983). The fear and loathing hypothesis suggests that people buy guns in response to their fear of crime and other incivilities present in our society. As such, individuals, fearful of elements of the larger society (e.g., crime and violence), go through a mental process where they begin to deplore crime, criminals, and the like and purchase firearms for protection. Several studies have attempted to test this hypothesis among adults with mixed results (Arthur 1992; Lizotte, Bordua, and White 1981; Smith and Uchida 1988; Wright and Marston 1975).

Recently, a number of researchers have diminished the loathing aspect of the hypothesis and have examined what May (1999) labeled the fear of criminal victimization hypothesis. Additionally, these researchers have utilized the fear of criminal victimization hypothesis to explain firearm possession and use among adolescents. Although protection is an oft-cited reason for weapon possession among adolescents, few studies attempt to examine the etiology of weapon possession for protection or the impact of fear of criminal victimization on weapon possession. Discussed below are those studies that: (1) examine predictors of weapon possession for protection; and (2) explicitly test (or at least attempt to test) the fear of criminal victimization hypothesis in explaining adolescent firearm possession.

Chandler et al. (1998), using data from a national sample of 23,933 students collected as part of the National Crime Victimization School Crime Supplement, determined that less than one percent of the sample carried a gun to school to protect themselves "from being attacked." They found that there were no statistically significant race, gender, or class differences in protective gun possession.

Lizotte et al. (1994), using data collected from a sample of 675 adolescent boys as part of the Rochester Youth Development Study in 1987-88, examined the causes of protective firearm *ownership*. Boys who admitted that they owned guns were asked whether they owned guns for sport or protection. Those who admitted that they owned guns for protection and those who admitted they owned guns for both protection and sport were classified as protective gun owners. Ten percent of the sample (67 boys) reported gun ownership; of that number, 30 reported ownership solely for protection while 10 stated that they owned guns for both protection and sport. Thus, 6% of the sample and 60% of the gun owners in the sample were categorized as protective gun owners.

Lizotte et al. (1994) determined that protective gun owners were more likely than those who did not own guns to be from lower income families, have delinquent values, engage in violent and gun crimes, use drugs, carry their guns regularly, and have peers who own guns. They suggest that protective gun ownership does not necessarily cause subsequent violent, firearm, and drug crime— it could be that the boys who own guns for protection obtain guns for protection and then find it more convenient to commit crime, or the need to own a gun for protection may have been brought about by prior delinquent activity. As Lizotte and his colleagues point out, it is difficult to unravel this relationship with cross-sectional data. Using responses from 656 boys collected as part of the same Rochester study used by Lizotte et al. (1994), Bjerregaard and Lizotte (1995) determined that gang members, blacks, and those who have peers who own guns are more likely to own guns for protection. Additionally, they determined that current gang members were more likely to own guns for protection than those who had once been in a gang but had ended their gang membership.

Webster et al. (1993) used data from a 1991 sample of 294 black junior high students in Washington D.C. Students were asked if they had "ever carried a gun with you for protection or to use in case you get into a fight" (1605). They were also asked another question worded in the exact same manner with the only exception being that the word "knife" was substituted for "gun." Nearly half of the males and just over one in three females had carried a knife for protection. One in four males and less than one in twenty females had carried a gun for protection. For both males and females, those who exhibited a greater tendency than classmates to get into fights, those who had been threatened or attacked with a knife or gun, those who had been arrested, and those who disagreed that having weapons increased injury risk were all more likely to carry knives for protection than their counterparts. Being threatened with a gun or knife did not have a significant effect upon protective firearm possession. Due to the fact that only six females had carried a gun, no models were estimated for that group (Webster et al. 1993).

While each of the aforementioned studies implies that some youths carry firearms or other weapons to school because they feel they need to be protected, none of those studies explicitly examine the impact of fear of criminal victimization on protective gun possession. Nevertheless, the realization that protective gun ownership and possession were prevalent among adolescents led others to explicitly examine the impact of fear of criminal victimization on firearm possession. Sheley and Brewer (1995) were the first researchers to test the fear of criminal victimization among a sample of adolescents. Using a sample of suburban high school students in Louisiana, they determined that fear had a nonsignificant association with carrying firearms *to school*, particularly for males. Their study was limited, however, by the fact that they used a single-item indicator of fear of criminal victimization, a method often criticized in the fear of crime literature (see Ferraro 1995, for a review).

Durant et al. (1997), using data collected from a sample of 3,054 public high school students in Boston, examined the relationship between weapon possession at school ("During the past thirty days, on how many days did you carry a weapon such as a gun, knife, or club?") and fear of school crime ("During the past thirty days, how many days did you not go to school because you felt you would be unsafe at school or on your way to or from school?") (362). After controlling for a number of other variables previously demonstrating a statistically significant association with weapon possession, they determined that students who had not attended school on six or more days in the previous month because of fear were over five times more likely to carry weapons to school (Durant et al. 1997).

May (1999) continued this line of research by examining the impact of fear of criminal victimization on firearm possession at school. Using a sample of over 7,000 public school students from Mississippi, he determined that students who perceived their neighborhoods as most disorderly and who were most fearful were significantly more likely to carry a gun to school. This association remained even after controlling for gang membership and theoretical measures of negative peer influence and attachment to family and school.

The most definitive test of the fear of criminal victimization was conducted by May (2001a). May attempted to replicate his findings from the previous study with a sample of almost 300 incarcerated adolescent males in Indiana. He did not find a statistically significant direct association between fear of criminal victimization and gun possession and use. He did, however, determine that those males who perceived themselves most at risk and whose neighborhoods were most criminogenic were more likely to carry guns. He suggests that, given the nature of his sample, that measures of perceptions of risk may be more indicative of support for the fear of criminal victimization hypothesis than measures of fear of criminal victimization, given the distinct likelihood that incarcerated adolescent males will not admit fear.

Other studies have also found partial support for the fear of criminal victimization hypothesis. For instance, Kingery, Pruitt, and Heuberger (1996) utilized data collected from eighth and tenth grade students in rural Texas to demonstrate that, among the 85 students who reported having carried a gun to school within twelve months of the survey, 48% stated that the reason was concern for safety. Other researchers have also determined that students who have been previously victimized at school are more likely to go to school armed (Kingery et al. 1996; Simon et al. 1999).

Nevertheless, there is little consensus regarding the impact of fear of criminal victimization on firearm possession among adolescents. Harris (1993, 15), in an analysis of data collected from 2,508 public and private school students across the United States, not only did not find evidence to support the fear of criminal victimization hypothesis but determined that youths who had carried a gun to school in the past thirty days were twice as likely *not* to be worried "about being in danger of being attacked physically" as their counterparts who had not carried a gun in the past thirty days. Other studies question the relationship between fear of criminal victimization and firearm possession as well (Bailey, Flewelling, and Rosenbaum 1997; Simon et al. 1997; Wilcox Rountree 2000). Finally, one other study showed victimization to be positively related to weapon carrying while the relationship between fear and in-school weapon carrying was null (Wilcox and Clayton 2001).

As the evidence presented above reveals, there is no consensus regarding the effectiveness of the fear of criminal victimization hypothesis in explaining adolescent firearm possession and use. While a number of youths admit that they carry firearms for protection, May (2001a) argues that these youths are carrying these weapons because of their perception that they are likely to be victimized, not necessarily due to their "fear" that they will be victimized. Further research is needed to clarify this relationship.

Firearm Possession and Use: Aggression?

Another latent result of fear of criminal victimization may be an increased propensity toward criminal behavior. It is possible that many youths believe that the risk they face in everyday interaction with others is so great that they need to take measures to protect themselves. These fearful individuals may carry weapons or take alternate measures to protect themselves and, consequently, the presence of a weapon may make the youths feel immune from victimization or retaliation. Thus, the availability of a firearm or other weapon may, in turn, incite aggressive behavior or even criminal activity from a person who fears that they are in danger. This relationship is often referred to as the "triggering effect" of firearm possession.

The "triggering effect" or "weapons effect" (Berkowitz and LePage 1967) implies that weapon carrying would lead to an increased risk of subsequent victimization. Further, it is also quite possible that the weapon carrier could be more likely to engage in violence because of the availability of the weapon. Recent work by Wells and Horney (2002, 283) shows that "compared with situations in which the respondent did not possess any weapon, both gun possession and other weapon possession increase the chances that the possessor will attack." So, from the standpoint of both offending and victimization, weapon carrying may serve to enhance the likelihood of subsequent violence.

It is also possible that the adolescent gun carrier may be more likely to engage in violence when carrying; further, protective firearm possession does not necessarily translate into a cognitive process whereby the firearm possessor limits himself or herself to firearm use only in protective situations. Wilcox (2002) suggests that there is no guarantee that protective gun possession will reduce the likelihood of victimization or the opportunity to engage in violence; in fact, she suggests that protective gun ownership might actually increase likelihood of future victimization (Wilcox 2002). In summary, while prior experience with crime is thought to precipitate protective firearm possession (and most previous work on the linkage assumes this temporal ordering—see May 2001a, for example), it is clear that the presence of a firearm (whether carried for protection or aggression) can, in turn, potentially influence experiences with crime in a variety of ways.

Motives for Protective Gun Possession

As described in chapter 3 and presented again in table 6.1, two in five respondents (41%) had carried a gun for protection at some point in their life. Additionally, almost half of the respondents (47%) had owned one or more guns in their life. Although over two-thirds of the respondents (68%) stated they never used a gun to commit a crime, one in ten (11%) had used a gun to commit a crime "once or twice" in their life, with slightly smaller percentages using a gun to commit a crime "a few times each year" (7%), and "a few times each month" (9%). One in twenty respondents (5%) used a gun to commit a crime "almost every day" prior to their incarceration. Thus, many of these respondents owned and carried guns and had used them in crimes as well.

Respondents who indicated that they had used a gun in a crime at least once in their life were then asked their motives for carrying a "gun or weapon other than a gun." While not a perfect measure of motivations for firearm possession, because we restrict this measure only to those who have used a gun in crime, we feel this measure provides a measure of motivations for why the respondents in this sample chose to carry a firearm. The results presented in table 6.2 suggest that the most important reasons for carrying a weapon among gun criminals were self-protective in nature. Over nine in ten gun criminals (93% and 92%, respectively) agreed that "you have to be ready to defend yourself" and "there is always the chance a victim might be armed" were either very important or somewhat important reasons why they carried a weapon. These findings replicate those of Sheley and Wright (1995), who determined that these two reasons were the most prevalent explanations among the youths who routinely carried guns during crime. Additionally, three in four respondents (74%) also felt that carrying a weapon made it less likely that people would "mess with" them, indicating a protective mindset as well.

The gun criminals also reported that carrying a weapon in a criminal transaction increased their likelihood for success, as four in five felt that having a weapon insured that "your victim doesn't put up a fight and you don't have to hurt them" (83%) and the presence of a weapon was helpful if they had a need to "escape from a situation" (80%). Thus, the gun criminals in this sample seem to believe that intimidation of their victim, while important, is not as important as their own protection. Both protection and intimidation, however, are far more important to this sample of respondents than status among their peers, as less than one in three respondents felt it was important to carry a weapon so that people would "respect" them (32%) or so their friends would not "look down" on them (28%).

Respondents were asked whether they had ever "carried a gun for protection." The model presented in table 6.3 depicts the results of a binomial logistic regression model regressing the responses to that question (hereafter referred to as protective gun carrying) on the demographic and contextual variables determined by previous researchers to have an association with protective gun possession (see chapter 2). The results presented in table 6.3 suggest that four variables had statistically significant associations with protective gun carrying. Males, nonwhites, youths from criminogenic neighborhoods, and gang members were significantly more likely to have carried a firearm for protection. None of the other variables included in the model had a statistically significant association with protective gun carrying.

These results thus provided limited support for the fear of criminal victimization hypothesis. The impact of protective gun carrying on race (nonwhites are typically more fearful) and being from a criminogenic neighborhood (whose residents are typically more fearful) support the hypothesis while the nonsignificant impact of victimization and perceptions of risk do not support the hypothesis. Nevertheless, both social learning and social disorganization theories would suggest that living in a criminogenic neighborhood makes one more likely to engage in all forms of crime and delinquency (see Vold, Bernard, and Snipes 1998). This fact, combined with the nonsignificant association between both actual and perceived victimization experience and protective gun carrying, suggests that any support for the fear of criminal victimization argument based on this association must be tempered at best.

If protective gun carrying were due solely to the impact of fear of criminal victimization, it would be counterintuitive to suggest that those youths who carry guns for protection would be more likely to engage in violent activity. In fact, the fear of criminal victimization hypothesis would argue that their fear of being victimized would make them avoid situations that increased their potential for victimization and, as such, fearful youths should be less likely to engage in violence. The data collected here allowed us the unique opportunity to test this effect and compare it to the "triggering effect" described earlier. Additionally, we were also able to include a measure of a tendency toward aggressive behavior as a control variable to determine if, after controlling for its effect, we can determine how much of the association between violence and protective gun carrying is independent of that tendency toward aggression. This tendency toward aggression was operationalized by responses to the statement "If someone insulted me, I would be likely to hit or slap them." Respondents who strongly agreed with that statement were assigned a score of 6 and those who strongly disagreed with that statement were assigned a score of 1.

Consequently, the results of regressing whether an individual had engaged in violent activity in their lifetime (described in chapter 2) on the demographic and contextual variables, protective gun carrying, and the measure of the respondent's tendency toward aggressive behavior are presented in table 6.4. The results indicate that those youths who had been victimized by crime were three (odds = 3.042) times more likely to engage in violence while those youths who had tendencies toward aggression were significantly more likely than their counterparts to have engaged in violent activity as well. Additionally, gang members were six (odds = 6.114) times more likely than non-gang members to have engaged in violent activity. Finally, those youths who had carried a gun for protection were over four (odds = 4.193) times more likely than youths who had not carried a gun for protection to engage in violent activity. None of the other variables had a statistically significant relationship with violent activity.

The results presented in table 6.4 offer substantial support for the triggering effect of protective gun carrying. Victims of violent threats, gang members, and those who carried guns for protection were all more likely to engage in at least one of the violent activities included in the index of violent activity.

Nevertheless, as discussed previously, based on the fact that the youths providing data for this study are far more violent than the typical sample of nonincarcerated youths, it could be that using a cumulative index may overestimate the triggering effect of protective gun ownership. As such, the results in table 6.5 depict the outcome of regressing whether a youth had "used force (strong-arm methods) to get money or things from people other than family members or schoolmates (hereafter referred to as robbery)" on the demographic and contextual variables, protective gun carrying, and the measure of the respondent's tendency toward aggressive behavior. We felt that using robbery as an outcome variable would allow for an improved test of the triggering effect in that those youths who had committed this crime had engaged in one of the most serious crimes (other than murder and rape, rare events even in this sample of violent youths) and, as such, could be considered the "most serious of the serious" offenders

The results indicate that those youths from criminogenic neighborhoods were significantly more likely to engage in robbery than their counterparts. Additionally, males were over four (odds = 4.454) times more likely to have robbed someone than females and those youths who had carried a gun for protection were almost three (odds = 2.908) times more likely than youths who had not carried a gun for protection to engage in robbery. Gang members were also significantly more likely to have robbed someone than those respondents who did not belong to gangs. Finally, those youths who perceived themselves most at risk of criminal victimization were also significantly more likely to have robbed someone as well. None of the other variables included in the model had a statistically significant association with robbery.

Qualitative Results

From the life-history data, we can provide examples of times that youths engaged in crimes while they were carrying guns. Lee describes why he and his friends were usually carrying guns on themselves:

> We just all started gettin' drunk and high. And then some more people came and people just kept comin' and then it started gettin' a little dark and everybody got to shootin' their guns off and stuff and havin' fun.
> *Was everyone just carrying their gun on them?*
> Yeah. 'Cause everybody, they can't really trust a whole lot of people 'cause if your sellin' drugs you might as well count on it 'cause a lot of people, they'll try to rob you.

Having his gun made it easy for Lee to take the steps he took when things started to get more exciting that same evening:

> I was with my girl and we was in there talkin' and then my buddy, R____, he came runnin' in and said, "someone just robbed me for his gun." And so I grabbed my gun and we ran outside and me and him, we got on some bicycles and we rode down the street and I seen the guy that robbed him. So then I pulled out my gun and I started shootin' at him and I shot the truck up that he was in. And then we ran, we ran back to my girl's house.

Later that same evening:

> We was all hangin' out. A gang more people came and the party was gettin' bigger. And then later on, these guys come by and they was wantin' to go do a robbery. And my buddy, he was needin' some money for his girl's birthday party the next day. I tried to give him the money so he wouldn't go get in trouble, but he didn't listen. So I was like, "I'm gonna go with you to back you up," 'cause I didn't trust the guys a whole lot that he was goin' to do it with. So we all got in the car and went ridin' around for a little bit. We smoked a little bit of weed while we was ridin' around and then one of the guys said he said he was gonna do it. So I took the gun out and I handed it to him and it was like two

blocks from the liquor store. And we all got out of the car and they said they was about to go do it so I sat up against the car, me and my friend, and two guys they went down to the liquor store. I seem 'em behind a barrel and then they went around it. It was like two minutes later they came runnin' out and came runnin' down the alley. I looked at my boy and I was like, "man, they did it." And then I asked 'em if they did and they was like, "yeah." And one of 'em said, "yeah and the police jumped out." And everybody ran and one of the guys, they jumped in the car and the car took off. And we all, like me, my friend and another dude, we all ran. We ran back to this apartment. We got back there and we was waitin' for them to pull up. They didn't pull up so we thought they got hit up by the police. So we just waited a little bit longer and they finally pulled up. He tried to hand me the gun back, but I told him not to give it to me. I told him to give it to my friend. So he gave it to my friend and they all went in the apartment and he pulled out, I think he pulled out a thousand, a thousand somethin' and he counted out some money for him and threw the rest on the floor. And this guy and my boy, they was in there splittin' it up and then I looked down, there's still some money down there so I went ahead and grabbed some of the money. I was gonna buy liquor with it.

Another subject, Ed, recounts an incident that occurred while he was carrying a handgun:

I was like 13 years old and there was this little skating club in my neighborhood and my momma used to let me go there. You just go there and skate and dance and stuff. A lot of girls would be there. So, plus my momma she knew the owners. They was like friends, you know what I mean? So I used to go there and I had a .25 and after it was over, me and my friend was walking in this parking lot, going home and wasn't causing no trouble or nothing. We had some girls walking with us, but a car kept veering like, driving crazy and was going in circles around us and just acting stupid, you know what I mean? So when the car finally stopped, the fool he pulled out a gun and put it to the window so everybody just stopped and I looked and I was like, man, so I tagged my friend and I'm like, "man, look at this dude, man." I'm like, "man this dude is crazy. He is going to kill us." So he sped off. He got to acting stupid and all this. So I was talking to this girl, man, and we was in the Walgreen parking lot and you know them stumps to where the car, where you park? Where you park and you have to stop? So we was standing on top of that, man, and the car just came real fast in front of us and hit the brakes and slid right and stopped in front of us and I looked and I'm like, "man." So I jumped off the bank to the sidewalk you know what I mean. The girl jumped off too. So the dude got out of the car and he like, "where my daughter at?" I'm, "man who's your daughter, man?" He was a big dude and I'm like, "who was your daughter?" I'm like, "I don't know your daughter." He just got to cursing and he grabbed me by my shoulder and I yanked away from him and then I pushed him. He was like, "oh, I got something for you," and he was trying to go to his car and I started shooting at him. Pow, pow. I mean, I start shooting. I mean, I could've killed him. I could've shot him basically 'cause I'm like right here. But I'm scared, you know what I mean. So I just started shooting at the car to let him know he better go ahead on. 'Cause as I was shooting I was running myself, you know what I mean? So I ran to these bushes and he jumped in the car and I was running. But I could've killed him. But I didn't. I just, I don't even know who this man was. I ain't even know his daughter. I think he was drunk, man.

In a different incident, Ed once again found himself in a position to need to use a gun that he was carrying:

We was like at a party and everybody, not everybody but some of us, was shooting dice. So I was shooting dice and my cousin had came in and he was like, "man, five dudes came here from ____. So everybody was in the kitchen and we all walked in the living room and got some dice from the living room. Well I'm looking at these dudes and they ain't saying nothing, so I ain't saying nothing. I guess they cool so to tell you the truth I don't know how it all started, but my friend, who got seven years now, him and one dude was in each others' face and so it was, like, a Puerto Rican dude had came with them. He had stood up and he grabbed his pocket and before he grabbed his pocket I grabbed him. Then I grabbed his pocket 'cause I thought he had a gun. So I grabbed his pocket and I was like, "man this is a wallet, he doesn't have no gun." So I'm like, "man, what the hell did you stand up for, man? What you about to do?" So he like, "no, I'm about to go out and get my boy, man" and all this. When he said that I looked at this dude and I looked back at him and his friend hit me. So I'm like, oh so I like put it to the dude and my friend they got to beating up the dude. You know what I'm saying? Some kind of way they got out of the house and got in they car. So my friend left to get in the car and they probably got somebody waiting on you. Well we pulled out the gun and you know what I'm saying we had them outside the car. They was scared and my friend was like, "kill them, kill them." I was like, I swear to God I started to laugh I was like, "no man, look at this dude. Man, he crying. Man, don't kill him. Man, don't kill him." Like one dude just fell to the floor calling on God, like "God please don't let them kill me." I swear. I uncocked the gun and I grabbed the dude and said, "come on man, I'm not going to kill you. "Get in your car and take your ass home, man."

As Edmundo suggests, there are criminal acts that happen because the youth was carrying a gun:

Are there crimes you've committed that you wish you hadn't done?
Yeah. Lots. Like shooting that guy in the back, shooting period. That just brings anger toward that person's hood, then they find out what hood we're in and start stuff with us. We've had to go to war with some hoods before and it was scary, so I wish I could have taken back those times. Just ever putting a gun in my hand. Really when I robbed, I had a gun in my hand. So I figured if I didn't have a gun, most of that stuff wouldn't have happened. Take back stealing some things.
Why would you take it back?
'Cause I really didn't need it, I just wanted it. I'm sure my parents would have given me money if I asked them for it

On the other hand, there are other instances of gun criminality in the life-history excerpts that appear to be the result of an aggressive intention, rather than a crime that happened incidentally while carrying a gun. For instance, Grant details a robbery that was planned out beforehand:

> The most violent [thing I ever did]? I don't know if I've told you about this or not, but the most violent would be when me and my boys, one of my friends, went up and, er, we didn't really kick down the door but we went in this dude's house and beat him up and took all of his money and his drugs and held him at gunpoint.
> That's probably the most violent thing I ever did.
> *Why did you guys do that?*
> Oh, let's see. I don't know, this lady lives next door and she's a crackhead and she told us where we could get a bunch of money and drugs from, but we were gonna have to steal it from the guy. So she took us over there, invited us in. We was playin' off, she was smokin' crack while we was there. I'd been there before and she told the dude that I was her brother so he let me in this time. My boy was with me and I said, "It's cool" and she said, "It's cool" so they let him in, but she's up there gettin' high and we're playin' it off like we're gonna buy a bunch of drugs from him 'cause we had money and everythin'. So she leaves, goes out. She says she has to go get her cigarettes or somethin' out of the car. I don't remember what it was. And she went down there and left us, 'cause she was supposed to be our getaway car. She left us. We didn't know that until we got down there, but there was somebody else that wanted to come buy drugs so they knocked on the door and he went back there sellin' their drugs while he was back there. My boy had a .380 pistol and I'm like, "you gotta either hit him with the pistol or knock him out with your first when he comes back out here." We didn't want to shoot nobody. So he's back there sellin' his drugs or whatever. The dude comes back. My friend hits him in his nose and the guy falls back and I grab him in a headlock. There was a dude in the kitchen that's gettin' high and this guy that I got in a headlock is screamin' and shit. So the dude in the kitchen runs out, runs out of the house. My friend starts checkin' the guys shorts and he keeps screamin' so I beat him up. I'm hittin' him and stuff and my friend gets the money. Well he finds a lot of money on the floor and then finds, like, I think it was 13 or 14 packs of crack cocaine that came out of his pockets, too. And my friend hits him real hard and knocks him out for a second and then he woke up and started screamin' and we uh, got the money and stuff. We ran out of the house and the guy was all bloody when we left

In another example, Casper details the motivation behind a drive-by shooting that does not appear to have happened spontaneously:

> The drive by was because they did something to one of my best friends. And they happened to be another gang member. So we were just getting revenge. For that one, I would not feel guilty if I shot a person.
> *What did they do? Did they shoot at your friend?*

Yeah. They tried to shoot him. He ran into the alley, if he didn't do that he would have gotten killed because there were like, two or three of them in the car.

In yet another case, Guy describes a scenario where he would commit a robbery that he planned out and selected a victim before he took an aggressive intentional action:

Did you ever use guns to commit crimes?
Yeah. When I robbed people out on the streets. If I seen this dude out all night selling dope and about two houses down and I seen him making all this money, man that's a quick $2000 to $3000. I would go to the crib, put my ski mask on and everything else, creep up on him and he would have it all. He would give me all. I would strip him down to where he wouldn't have nothing but his boxers on and make him walk.
Why strip him down?
Make sure he doesn't have a gun so when I leave, he can't shoot me.
What did you do with his clothes?
I just threw them. If he had a gun I kept the gun.

Is Gun Possession a Protective or Aggressive Activity?

The results presented in this chapter reveal a number of interesting findings. First and foremost, the incarcerated youths providing data for this study were accustomed to a lifestyle that included firearm possession. Two in five respondents had carried a gun for protection in their life and almost half of the sample had owned a gun. One in twenty carried a gun almost every day before they were incarcerated and one in ten carried a gun a few times each month. As such, these youths have an intimate familiarity with firearms not often found in samples of public school youths. Additionally, the youths who had used guns in crime admitted that they used a gun in crime for two reasons: to protect themselves from harm and to increase their chances of a successful criminal transaction.

The results presented in this chapter also suggest that males, nonwhites, older youths, youths from criminogenic neighborhoods, and gang members were those youths who were most likely to have carried a gun for protection. Coupled with the qualitative data, these findings lend partial support for the fear of criminal victimization hypothesis. Nevertheless, the examination of violent activities and robbery tends to suggest that protective gun carrying may have a triggering effect for violent activity. Those youths who had carried guns for protection and gang members were significantly more likely to have engaged in both violent activity in general and robbery. These two variables were the only two that predicted both general violent activity and robbery. Being a victim of violent threats and having a higher likelihood to respond to a situation aggressively predict violent activity in general, but not robbery; males and those youths from criminogenic neighborhoods are significantly more likely to engage in robbery but not violent activity in general. Being nonwhite and being older appears to predict protective gun carrying but has little impact on either violent activity or robbery in this sample. Receiving public assistance does not predict a greater likelihood of any of the activities in this chapter.

Tables

TABLE 6.1 Characteristics of gun possession

	N	%
Have you ever carried a gun for protection?		
Yes	325	40.7
No	473	59.3
How many guns have you ever owned?		
0	437	52.8
1 or more	391	47.2
Before you came to this facility, about how often did you use a gun to commit a crime?		
Almost every day	45	5.4
A few times each month	77	9.3
A few times each year	55	6.6
Only once or twice in my life	88	10.6
Never	563	68.0

TABLE 6.2 Reasons gun criminals carry firearms

Reason for carrying weapon	Very/Somewhat Important N (%)	Not Important N (%)
If I am planning a crime, there is always a chance a victim might be armed.	241 (92.3)	20 (7.7)
You have to be ready to defend yourself.	242 (93.1)	18 (6.9)
If you have a weapon when you commit a crime, your victim doesn't put up a fight and you don't have to hurt them.	214 (83.3)	43 (16.7)
I feel I might need a weapon to escape from a situation.	208 (80.0)	52 (20.0)
People just don't mess with you when you have a weapon.	191 (73.5)	69 (26.5)
In my crowd, if you don't have a gun, people don't respect you.	84 (32.4)	175 (67.6)
My friends would look down on me if I did not carry a gun.	72 (27.8)	187 (72.2)

TABLE 6.3 Multivariate logistic regression results on whether respondent had ever carried a gun for protection

Predictor	B	S.E.	Wald	Exp(B)
Public assistance recipient	-.043	.202	.045	.958
Male	1.129	.268	17.725***	3.093
Nonwhite	.416	.192	4.673*	1.516
Age	.143	.077	3.488	1.154
Perceived neighborhood incivility	.085	.015	33.316***	1.089
Victim of violent threats	.145	.241	.365	1.157
Perceptions of risk index	.168	.099	2.861	1.182
Gang member	1.659	.193	74.012***	5.252
Constant	-6.300			
Chi-Square	238.517***			
-2 Log Likelihood	699.828			
Nagelkerke R-Square	.392			

* p<.05   ** p<.01   *** p<.001

TABLE 6.4. Multivariate logistic regression results on whether respondent had engaged in violent activity

Predictor	B	S.E.	Wald	Exp(B)
Public assistance recipient	-.064	.253	.064	.938
Male	.442	.256	2.973	1.555
Nonwhite	-.411	.242	2.889	.663
Age	.146	.093	2.431	1.157
Perceived neighborhood incivility	.031	.019	2.564	1.032
Victim of violent threats	1.112	.258	18.563***	3.042
Perceptions of risk index	.135	.131	1.066	1.145
Likelihood of aggression	.201	.071	7.933**	1.222
Protective gun carrier	1.433	.375	14.624***	4.193
Gang member	1.811	.405	19.955***	6.114
Constant	-3.791			
Chi-Square	171.252***			
-2 Log Likelihood	474.321			
Nagelkerke R-Square	.367			

* p<.05   ** p<.01   *** p<.001

Gun Possession: Protection or Aggression

TABLE 6.5 Multivariate logistic regression results on whether respondent had ever committed robbery

Predictor	B	S.E.	Wald	Exp(B)
Public assistance recipient	-.042	.206	.042	.959
Male	1.494	.333	20.177***	4.454
Nonwhite	-.261	.197	1.757	.771
Age	-.022	.077	.079	.979
Perceived neighborhood incivility	.042	.015	7.623**	1.043
Victim of violent threats	.240	.252	.913	1.272
Perceptions of risk index	.289	.097	8.900**	1.335
Likelihood of aggression	.055	.062	.777	1.057
Protective gun carrier	1.068	.214	24.928***	2.908
Gang member	.468	.211	4.939*	1.597
Constant	-3.681			
Chi-Square	163.290***			
-2 Log Likelihood	680.828			
Nagelkerke R-Square	.298			

* $p<.05$ ** $p<.01$ *** $p<.001$

CHAPTER 7

Theoretical Predictors of Protective Gun Carrying, Violent Activity, and Gun Use in Crime

In previous chapters, we examined from where juveniles obtain their guns, what types of guns they prefer, and why juveniles choose the guns they do. Additionally, we have attempted to explain whether juvenile gun possession is an aggressive or a defensive act. Our findings have not ruled out the possibility that gun possession (whether for protection or not) is just one of a wide variety of activities in which delinquent youths engage and is caused by the same factors that contribute to delinquency that is not gun-related. As such, we feel that it is important to attempt to isolate the impact of gun possession on delinquency, controlling for other factors commonly related to delinquency.

Theoretical Explanations of Delinquency

In this chapter, we examine four theoretical predictors of delinquency. Three of the theoretical perspectives (strain theory, differential association theory, and social bond theory) have demonstrated an association with delinquency in a wide variety of settings and activities; the other (nonsocial reinforcement theory) is a relatively new theoretical perspective but has received some empirical support as well. Each of the theoretical perspectives is discussed in detail below.

Differential Association Theory

One of the most widely recognized theoretical explanations of crime and delinquency is Edwin Sutherland's differential association theory. Sutherland first posited his idea of differential association theory in 1939. Since that time, numerous researchers have examined its efficacy in predicting criminal behavior and Sutherland's ideas have received wide support.

Sutherland's (1947, 6-8) theory of differential association is founded on nine basic principles. Below, each of the principles is cited verbatim from Sutherland's fourth revision of his original work (*in italics*), followed by a contemporary explanation of the principle in our own words. These principles are as follows:

1. *Criminal behavior is learned.* Individuals learn criminal behavior in much the same manner that they learn noncriminal behavior.

2. *Criminal behavior is learned in interaction with other persons in a process of communication.* Individuals who violate the law learn to do so from other individuals and settings where they are socialized into criminal behavior. Thus, some individuals can be raised in a criminogenic environment yet refrain from delinquency and criminal behavior.

3. *The principle part of the learning of criminal behavior occurs within intimate personal groups.* Criminal behavior is learned from those people with whom an individual has the most intimate relationships. These groups include family members, peers, and friends. Thus, if an individual is exposed to criminal behavior among family and friends, that youth is more likely to engage in crime and delinquency.

4. *When criminal behavior is learned, the learning includes (a) techniques of committing the crime, which are sometimes very complicated, sometimes very simple; (b) the specific direction of motives, drives, rationalizations, and attitudes.* As individuals interact with these intimate personal groups, these youths learn the techniques for committing crime (e.g., how to break into a car as quickly as possible, identifying characteristics of undercover law enforcement officers when engaging in drug transactions). They develop motives and attitudes that make them more likely to engage in criminality. They also develop justifications and rationalizations that allow them to continue to engage in criminal behavior.

5. *The specific direction of motives and drives is learned from definitions of the legal codes as favorable or unfavorable.* Youths who engage in crime do so because socialization experiences with their family and friends have caused them to develop a negative attitude toward many of the existing laws. This negative attitude leads the individual to feel that, because these laws are unfair or unjust, the codes should not apply to their own behavior.

6. *A person becomes delinquent because of an excess of definitions favorable to violation of law over definitions unfavorable to violations of law.* Sutherland suggests that individuals become criminal when, through the process of socialization with their intimate personal groups, the definitions unfavorable to law outweigh the definitions favorable to law that they have learned from the larger society.

7. *Differential associations may vary in frequency, duration, priority, and intensity.* Sutherland suggests that an individual's decision to obey or disobey the law is also affected by qualities of their interactions with

intimate personal groups. Those interactions that occur most frequently have more impact on an individual's behavior than those that occur less frequently. Those interactions that last the longest amount of time have more impact on the individual than those that last for a brief period of time. Sutherland further suggests that those interactions that occur early in life (priority) are likely to have more influence than those that occur later in life and those interactions that produce the most emotional reward for an individual (intensity) have the strongest impact on an individual's behavior.

8. *The process of learning criminal behavior by association with criminal and anti-criminal patterns involves all the mechanisms that are involved in any other learning.* Learning criminal behavior patterns involves many of the same processes as learning noncriminal behavior patterns. Thus, learning how and why to steal a car is much like learning how to drive a car.

9. *While criminal behavior is an expression of general needs and values, it is not explained by these needs and values, since non-criminal behavior is an expression of the same needs and values.* Sutherland suggests that motives for criminal behavior are different than those for conformist behavior. As such, many of the antecedents of crime posited by other theorists (e.g., poverty, low self-control, school failure) are not causes of crime because they are just as likely to produce conformist behavior as they are criminal behavior (e.g., working hard to get a good job, using a tutor to increase school performance). Sutherland suggests that only the learning of deviant definitions and norms through contact with intimate personal groups makes individuals engage in crime and delinquency.

In sum, Sutherland argues that individuals engage in crime and delinquency because they associate with actors in intimate personal groups that have attitudes and activities that are favorable to criminality. In these intimate personal groups, individuals learn motives, attitudes, and definitions that make them more likely to engage in criminal behavior than their counterparts whose intimate personal groups have conformist beliefs and behaviors. A number of theorists have conducted empirical tests of differential association theory and many have found empirical support for most of its tenets (Matsueda 1982; Matsueda and Heimer 1987; Tittle, Burke, and Jackson 1986). Association with delinquent peers has also demonstrated a strong relationship with delinquent behavior (Cao and Deng 1998; Farrington and Loeber 2000; Gottfredson 2001; Johnson, Marcos, and Bahr 1987).

Social Bond Theory

Social bond theory is most often associated with Travis Hirschi (1969). Hirschi's social bond theory emerged out of the social control theoretical perspective, which suggests that all people would commit crime if there were not "controlling forces" that restrain an individual from engaging in crime (Vold,

Bernard, and Snipes 1998). The emergence of the social control perspective can be traced to works by Reiss (1951), Nye (1958), and Reckless (1961), all of whom suggested that individuals refrain from engaging in delinquency because of internal and/or external controls that help them resist the urge to engage in nonconformist behavior. External controls include factors such as family, school, and church while internal controls include a positive self-image and a good self-concept. Youths who have good external and internal control systems thus are less likely to engage in delinquency (Cao 2004; Vold, Bernard, and Snipes 1998).

In his book *Causes of Delinquency*, Hirschi (1969) developed what is now referred to as "social bond" theory. Hirschi argues that we are all capable of committing criminal acts; only those individuals who have a strong social bond and attachment to society and social institutions (such as the school and the family) refrain from delinquent acts. According to Hirschi, there are four elements of the social bond: involvement, belief, attachment, and commitment. Attachment is the most important element of the social bond and is the element necessary for internalizing the norms and values of a society. According to Hirschi, youths who are attached to society have effective ties to school, family, and friends and are sensitive to the needs of others in society. Belief is the extent to which people believe in the society's moral validity and laws. Adolescents who firmly believe that societal laws are designed in the best interest of themselves and others in society are less likely to engage in crime and delinquency. Commitment is the stake an individual has in conformity and what that person stands to lose by committing a crime. The higher the stake, the less likely the individual is to commit crime. Thus, youths who are actively engaged in school-related and/or church-related activities are less likely to engage in delinquency. Finally, involvement is the degree to which a youth participates in conformist activities (e.g., having a job, engaging in extracurricular activities). Hirschi (1969) argues that a strong bond with society reduces the likelihood that the juvenile will become delinquent. Although some authors question the efficacy of some aspects of social control theory (Greenberg 1999; Miller, Esbensen, and Freng 1999) a number of studies have confirmed Hirschi's ideas (Cernkovich and Giordano 1979a, 1979b, 1987, 1992; Rankin and Kern 1994).

Strain Theory

The emergence of strain theory can be traced most directly to the work of Robert Merton (1938). Merton suggested that each individual in a society develops a goal system based on the culture of the larger society. In American society, the most prominent goal is to acquire wealth. In fact, Merton suggests that the American culture emphasizes financial wealth above all other goals. Consequently, those that are unable to achieve the goal of financial wealth are often devalued in the American society (Merton 1938). Despite this overarching emphasis on the goal of financial wealth in the United States, Merton suggests that not everyone has the same ability to achieve that goal. Instead, that societal structure, by limiting the abilities of certain groups to achieve the goal of financial wealth, puts pressure on those groups to engage in deviant activity to achieve financial wealth (Merton 1938).

Merton (1938) also emphasized that each culture develops its own institutionalized means for accomplishing the cultural goals. Thus, in the United States, the institutionalized means included hard work, honesty, deferred gratification, and education. Societal members are expected to use these institutionalized means to accomplish financial wealth. Those who conform to these goals, yet do not achieve financial wealth, receive little social reward for adhering to these means. Nevertheless, people who achieve the goal of financial wealth, even if they use unapproved means, often receive the prestige and social status that come with financial wealth. As such, Merton suggests that this places a severe "strain" on those who cannot achieve wealth through institutionalized means. This strain is often concentrated among persons in the lower class because the means to achieve the goal of financial wealth are often limited by societal structure in a capitalistic system.

Merton suggests that when societies have the aforementioned imbalanced emphasis on achievement of goals on one hand and the use of institutionalized means on the other, anomie results. Anomie is pervasive in a society when societies emphasize a common goal such as wealth for the entire population but do not provide equal access to legitimate means to achieve that goal. As such, Merton suggests that some individuals adapt to that anomic condition by engaging in crime, or using illegitimate means (Merton 1938).

Merton (1938) created a typology of adaptations to anomie within a society. These adaptations include: (1) conformists, or those who accept the institutionalized means to achieve the cultural goal of financial wealth; (2) innovators, or those who reject the institutionalized means to achieve the cultural goal of financial wealth; (3) ritualists, or those who reject the cultural goal of financial wealth but continue to accept the institutionalized means of the society; (4) retreatists, or those who reject both the cultural goals of financial wealth and the institutionalized means to achieve those goals; and (5) rebels, or those who reject both the cultural goal of financial wealth and the institutionalized means to achieve those goals and seek to reorder both the cultural goals of society and the institutionalized means to achieve those goals. According to Merton (1938), most crime, particularly instrumental types of crime such as robbery and burglary, is committed by innovators. A number of theorists have attempted to expand and enhance Merton's theory of anomie. The three most prominent schools of thought were developed by Cloward and Ohlin (1960), Cohen (1955), and Agnew (1992). Although Cohen's version predates that of Cloward and Ohlin and Agnew, Cohen's version will be discussed last and in most detail as it is most applicable to this study.

Cloward and Ohlin (1960) sought to synthesize the ideas of Merton with those of social disorganization theorists and social learning theorists like Sutherland. Cloward and Ohlin agreed with Merton that some members of society were denied access to the legitimate means to achieve the goal of financial wealth. Nevertheless, while they concur that a set of approved means exists to achieve cultural goals, they suggest that illegitimate avenues also exist and that in urban, lower class areas where legitimate means are limited, some youths will engage in opportunities of a different (illegitimate) kind to achieve the goal of financial wealth. Cloward and Ohlin thus argue that lower class youths, whose legitimate opportunities are limited, join delinquent subcultures to pursue the goal of financial wealth through illegitimate means. This perspective has become known as differential opportunity theory. Differential opportunity theorists argue that strain exists in the lower class and youths will join one of three types of gangs (criminal gangs, conflict gangs, or retreatist gangs) to adapt to that strain (Cloward and Ohlin 1960).

Agnew (1992) began a series of articles where he outlined the basis for what has come to be known as general strain theory. In an effort to expand strain theory to explain negative relationships other than those caused by lack of access to legitimate means to meet valued goals, Agnew argues crime and delinquency result from negative affective states caused by negative emotions generated from negative relationships with others. Agnew suggests that there are psychological and emotional adaptations to strain that are elicited from these negative relationships. Agnew suggests that strain originates from three sources: (1) Relationships where an individual prohibits another from achieving a valued goal; (2) Relationships where something a person has that is valued is taken away; and (3) Relationships where something is imposed on a person that is unwanted (Agnew 1992). Agnew argues that each type of relationship has the potential to elicit a number of negative emotions (such as fear, depression, and anger) and these negative emotions may cause delinquency. A number of his recent works have supported this thesis (Agnew 2001; Agnew et al. 2002; Agnew and White 1992).

While both Cloward and Ohlin and Agnew have extended (and to some extent) synthesized strain theory with other theoretical perspectives, Cohen's (1955) extension of strain theory is the one that remains closest to the anomic tradition that Merton worked within. Cohen (1955) suggests that most delinquency occurs as part of a group effort among adolescents and is often non-utilitarian (serves no apparent purpose). Further, Cohen argues that lower class boys engage in these behaviors not to obtain financial wealth, as Merton suggests, but to gain prestige and status among their peers. He argues that a delinquent subculture emerges through a process of adaptations by youths to what they perceive as blocked access to middle-class status.

Consequently, unable to meet middle-class standards, some lower-class adolescents become alienated and ostracized from conventional society. Further, some of these youths come to share perceptions of an unjust society and, collectively, these youths realize that they have the similar problem of status attainment. Consequently, the delinquent subculture allows these youths to reduce "strain" by allowing them to gain status through their delinquent activities (Cohen 1955).

This alternative value system allows the member of these delinquent subcultures to acquire prestige by way of delinquency. Delinquency is also the social mechanism to relieve frustration or pressure resulting from the inability to compete effectively with middle-class students in the school environment. Cohen (1955) argues that these acts in which members of the delinquent subculture engage are "non-utilitarian, malicious and negativistic" (Cohen 1955, 25). Although Cohen does not assert that delinquency is entirely a group phenomenon, he does contend that a large amount of delinquency occurs in groups.

Thus, Cohen (1955) suggests that many youths engage in crime and delinquency because of their perception that they do not have the same opportunities as others to obtain "middle class" status. As such, the delinquent activities in which these youths engage are a result of their perceptions of blocked opportunities. Despite differences in methodologies, particularly in the methods of operationalizing blocked opportunities, a number of research efforts have supported this argument (Baron and Hartnagel 1997; Cernkovich 1978; Cernkovich and Giordano 1979; Simons and Gray 1989; Vowell and May 2000)

Nonsocial Reinforcement Theory

Recently, some researchers have moved away from the idea that delinquent behavior stems from association with deviant peers, weak social bonds, or feelings of strain and have begun to examine the relationship between intrinsic satisfaction received from engagement in risky behavior and involvement in delinquency. Drawing upon a number of studies from the field of social psychology that suggest intrinsic satisfaction is an important predictor of delinquent behavior (e.g., Grasmick and Bursik 1990; Gove and Wilmoth 1990; Moore and Rosenthal 1993). Wood et al. (1995) introduced the idea of nonsocial reinforcement theory.

Nonsocial reinforcement theory is an extension and reformulation of social learning theory. Like traditional social learning theory and, to some extent, differential association theory, nonsocial reinforcement theorists maintain that individuals continue to participate in deviant behavior because of the rewards they receive from that participation. Nonsocial reinforcement theorists, however, argue that the reward comes not from external but internal stimuli. Wood et al. (1997) contend that most people who continue to engage in deviance do so because they find the acts to be "intrinsically pleasurable," obtaining this pleasure from a combination of the neurophysical "high" the behavior produces (e.g., adrenaline for theft, altered state of mind for marijuana and alcohol) and the symbolic meaning of the act (Wood et al. 1997). Thus, nonsocial reinforcement theorists argue that individuals who engage in deviant behavior do so because of the intrinsic reinforcement they receive from the act, not from the social reward they receive from their peers.

Wood et al. (1995) suggested that thrill seeking and immediate gratification had strong, statistically significant influences on illegal drug and alcohol use among adolescents. They found that immediate gratification was the strongest predictor of frequency of marijuana and hard drug use. Thus, nonsocial reinforcement theory does appear to have a significant influence on at least some delinquent behavior. May (2003), May, Nichols, and Eltzroth (1998), and Arnett (1995) have presented results consistent with this effect.

Each of the four theoretical perspectives reviewed above has been demonstrated to impact a wide variety of deviant and delinquent activities in a wide variety of settings. Nevertheless, to our knowledge, no researchers have ever examined the four theoretical perspectives concurrently to predict either: (a) weapon usage in crime; or (b) violent activity specifically. As such, this effort expands the knowledge in this area by examining the impact of these theoretical perspectives on violent and weapon-related delinquency.

Theoretical Predictors of Gun Criminality and Violence

We were first interested in whether the theoretical perspectives considered here had a statistically significant impact on whether the youths in this sample had ever carried a gun for protection. Using the dichotomous measure of protective gun carrying described earlier, we regressed whether or not the youths had carried a gun for protection on the demographic and contextual variables, the measure of the respondent's tendency toward aggressive behavior, and the four indices representing the theoretical perspectives described above (the measures used to comprise the indices are included in Chapter 2). The results from that logistic regression model are presented in table 7.1.

The results presented in table 7.1 indicate that males were over three times (3.350) more likely to carry guns for protection than females while nonwhites were 1.7 times more likely to carry guns for protection than whites. Additionally, gang members were almost five times (4.854) more likely than youths who did not belong to gangs to have carried a gun for protection. Those youths whose neighborhoods were most criminogenic were also significantly more likely than their counterparts to have carried a gun for protection. With the exception of the index representing nonsocial reinforcement theory, the indices representing the theoretical perspectives under study here did not have a significant association with whether the youths had carried a gun for protection. Youths with greater tendencies toward risky behavior were significantly more likely to have carried a gun for protection than their counterparts.

Our interest then turned to examining whether the respondents have ever committed a crime with a gun. Using the dichotomous measure of gun criminal described in chapter 6, we regressed whether or not the youths had committed a crime with a gun on the demographic and contextual variables, protective gun carrying, the measure of the respondent's tendency toward aggressive behavior, and the four indices representing the theoretical perspectives. These results are presented in table 7.2.

The results presented in table 7.2 indicate that males were two times (2.002) more likely to have used a gun in crime than females while those youths whose neighborhoods were most criminogenic and who perceived themselves most at risk of victimization were also significantly more likely than their counterparts to have committed a crime with a gun. Additionally, gang members were almost three (2.836) times more likely than those who were not gang members to have used a gun in crime while those youths who had carried a gun for protection were over six (6.105) times more likely than youths who had not carried a gun for protection to commit a crime with a gun. With the exception of the index representing differential association, the indices representing the theoretical perspectives under study here did not have a significant association with whether the youths had used a gun in a criminal act. Youths whose friends were least likely to disapprove of deviant behavior were significantly more likely to engage in violent activity than their counterparts.

The results presented in table 7.2 provide even greater support for a triggering effect of protective gun carrying than those presented in chapter 6. Protective gun carriers were six times more likely to have used a gun in crime than those youths who had not carried a gun for protection, even after controlling for theoretical perspectives that often have a statistically significant association with all types of delinquency.

The results of regressing whether an individual had engaged in violent activity in their lifetime on the demographic and contextual variables, protective gun carrying, the measure of the respondent's tendency toward aggressive behavior, and the four indices representing the theoretical perspectives described above are presented in table 7.3. The results indicate that gang members were over five (5.613) times more likely to engage in violent activity than non-gang members, while those youths who had been victimized by crime were almost three (2.929) times more likely to engage in violence than their counterparts who had not faced violent threats. Those youths who had tendencies toward aggression were significantly more likely than their counterparts to have engaged in violent activity as well. Finally, those youths who had carried a gun for protection were almost four (3.987) times more likely than youths who had not carried a gun for protection to engage in violent activity. With the exception of the index representing differential association, the indices representing the theoretical perspectives under study here did not have a significant association with violent activity. Youths whose friends were least likely to disapprove of deviant behavior were significantly more likely to engage in violent activity than their counterparts.

Consequently, the results presented in table 7.3 continue to offer substantial support for the triggering effect of protective gun carrying. Gang members, youths who were victims of violent threats, and those who carried guns for protection were all more likely to engage in at least one of the violent activities included in the index of violent activity, even after controlling for the impact of four of the more well-regarded theoretical perspectives. Differential association appeared to be the only theoretical perspective that had any success in predicting violent activity among this sample.

The results presented in table 7.4 depict the outcome of regressing whether a youth had engaged in robbery on the demographic and contextual variables, protective gun carrying, and indices representing the four theoretical perspectives. The results indicate that males were over four (4.522) times more likely to have robbed someone than females and those youths who had carried a gun for protection were almost three (2.808) times more likely than youths who had not carried a gun for protection to engage in violent activity. Additionally, those youths who perceived themselves to be most at risk of criminal victimization and gang members were also significantly more likely to have robbed someone as well. None of the other demographic or contextual variables included in the model had a statistically significant association with robbery.

Perhaps the most interesting finding presented in this chapter concerns the relationship between robbery and the theoretical perspectives. Whereas differential association theory and nonsocial reinforcement theories were the only statistically significant predictors of protective gun possession, violent activity, and using a gun in crime, neither had a statistically significant association with robbery in this study. In contrast, youths in this sample who were least "attached to school" (least likely to consider school an enjoyable experience) and experiencing the most "strain" (most likely to feel that they would not have the same opportunities for success as their counterparts) were significantly more likely to have engaged in robbery in their lifetime. As such, the robbery appears to have a different theoretical etiology than either carrying a gun for protection, using a gun in crime, or violent activity in general.

Qualitative Results

The life-history interviews provide some examples of the role that differential association plays in the involvement of delinquent youths with guns. Edmundo provides an incident in which his peers encouraged him to carry out a crime with a gun:

> When I was about 14 years old we were walking down Delaware and we came to 35th and there was a church there, it was shut down and there was an old man walking and there was a lady coming this way. We were sitting on the steps of the church and we could see the lady holding money and counting it and putting it in her purse. So I was like, "I'm about to rob her," and they were like, "do it, do it, do it!"
> *Was that the first time you robbed somebody?*
> I think that was my first time. So we all ran to T___'s house, fast, and grabbed some masks and passed the church and then started walking. She passed Delaware and crossed the street and kept going. I ran like two alleys down and I grabbed her and carried her like half way down the block. She was kicking and punching and I was holding her arms from like here to her elbows and I had her back against my chest and ran. I didn't think I was strong enough, but I did. I carried her all the way down to the dumpster, and then I pulled my gun out and said, "just give me your money." She did it. She just threw me her purse basically and I was going to keep her credit cards, but I was like, no. I had my gloves on and I was looking through her wallet.
> *What were the gloves for?*
> Fingerprints.
> *You just had those on you?*
> No, we went back to T___'s before that and got the mask and gloves.

And the gun, did you get that there too?
No, I had the gun. So I looked through her purse and there was about $400 in there. I was like, "thank you" and threw her purse down and I was like, "sorry." Then I ran down the alley and I went to the woods and stayed there and hid, but really the police never came looking. She turned out to be a crackhead because my boy used to sell dope to her.

Robert recounts another incident in which his negative peers influenced him to get involved with criminal activity involving a gun:

I was running with the good crowd but I still had my friends from the year before. I still talked to them and one of them came up to me and they had a gun. They had a small little gun or whatever and they wanted to break into the house next to me. Since it was a duplex they knew I had the key

Other life-history narratives provide us with gun-related anecdotes in support of nonsocial reinforcement theory. For instance, Ed describes the attraction that guns had for him:

I don't want to say I'm fascinated by guns, man, but like now I hate guns you know what I...I don't hate them but I'm not so quick to pick up a gun now. You know what I mean? But at the time, I don't know. I don't care where we going man. I got to have a gun. I just, I don't want to say I was fascinated but I just liked guns I guess.
Did you always carry a gun on you?
(Shook his head yes)
Where would you carry it?
In my back pocket.

Could people tell it was a gun?
I don't know. Yeah I guess.
Did you see people walking with guns in their back pockets?
Yeah.
Can you sit with it in there?
Yeah I mean it will pull your pants down, some. Sometime I have it on my side. If I had a coat like if it was dark outside it's going to be like in my pocket, my front pocket or something like that. But I don't know man, I like guns, man. I did 'cause, I like, I don't know.
What about them?
Boom!
You like that?
Yeah.

Guy puts it another way:

All violence does is lead you to trouble. I mean at the time it seems fun. Like breaking into a person's house. That's a rush, that's an adrenaline rush. Shooting a gun at somebody it is just like, if you are in a shoot out you are so scared to get shot, you're shooting at them, that's it. If you shoot and kill them you don't have to worry about getting shot, that's how it is. I've done been in so many gun fights it's not funny.

You get a rush out of that?

A terrified rush. I mean, you don't want to be in it but it's like I'm going to shoot you and kill you before you shoot and kill me, that's the way it is.

Conclusion

The results presented in this chapter provide strong support for the triggering effect when it comes to the relationship between gun carrying and violent activity. Protective gun carriers were far more likely to: (a) have used a gun in crime; (b) have engaged in violent activity; and (c) have engaged in robbery. This statistically significant impact remained, even after controlling for theoretical perspectives often found to explain all types of delinquency. In the following chapter, we discuss the implications of this effect for policies designed to reduce both gun violence and violent activity in general.

Tables

TABLE 7.1. Multivariate logistic regression results on whether respondent had ever carried a gun for protection

Predictor	B	S.E.	Wald	Exp(B)
Public assistance recipient	-.031	.207	.022	.969
Male	1.209	.277	19.089***	3.350
Nonwhite	.519	.205	6.432*	1.681
Age	.150	.078	3.76	1.162
Perceived neighborhood incivility	.070	.016	19.062***	1.073
Victim of violent threats	.090	.245	.135	1.094
Perceptions of risk index	.139	.101	1.894	1.149
Differential association index	.123	.120	1.053	1.131
Nonsocial reinforcement index	-.312	.112	7.702**	.732
Social control index	-.013	.115	.013	.987
Strain index	-.049	.113	.185	.952
Gang member	1.580	.196	65.226***	4.854
Constant	-1.178			
Chi-Square	251.044***			
-2 Log Likelihood	687.300			
Nagelkerke R^2	.409			

* p<.05   ** p<.01   *** p<.001

TABLE 7.2 Multivariate logistic regression results on whether respondent had ever committed a crime with a gun

Predictor	B	S.E.	Wald	Exp(B)
Public assistance recipient	-.385	.232	2.757	.680
Male	.694	.311	4.995*	2.002
Nonwhite	.485	.229	4.503*	1.624
Age	-.158	.087	3.274	.854
Perceived neighborhood incivility	.040	.018	4.946*	1.041
Victim of violent threats	.012	.268	.002	1.012
Perceptions of risk index	.217	.106	4.181*	1.242
Likelihood of aggression	.002	.072	.001	1.002
Protective gun carrier	1.809	.227	63.660***	6.105
Differential association index	.267	.134	3.971*	1.306
Nonsocial reinforcement index	-.130	.127	1.056	.878
Social control index	.134	.125	1.143	1.143
Strain index	-.019	.126	.024	.981
Gang member	1.042	.220	22.462***	2.836
Constant	-1.178			
Chi-Square	294.924***			
-2 Log Likelihood	585.287			
Nagelkerke R^2	.482			

* p<.05   ** p<.01   *** p<.001

TABLE 7.3 Multivariate logistic regression results on whether respondent had engaged in violent activity

Predictor	B	S.E.	Wald	Exp(B)
Public assistance recipient	-.044	.258	.029	.957
Male	.497	.264	3.532	1.643
Nonwhite	-.261	.254	1.056	.770
Age	.152	.095	2.547	1.164
Perceived neighborhood incivility	.015	.021	.526	1.015
Victim of violent threats	1.075	.262	16.786***	2.929
Perceptions of risk index	.123	.132	.877	1.131
Likelihood of aggression	.176	.075	5.505*	1.193
Protective gun carrier	1.383	.376	13.531***	3.987
Differential association index	.345	.140	6.082*	1.412
Nonsocial reinforcement index	-.117	.138	.722	.890
Social control index	-.074	.140	.278	.929
Strain index	-.001	.140	.000	.999
Gang member	1.725	.409	17.783***	5.613
Constant	-3.510			
Chi-Square	179.913***			
-2 Log Likelihood	465.660			
Nagelkerke R^2	.383			

* p<.05   ** p<.01   *** p<.001

TABLE 7.4 Multivariate logistic regression results on whether respondent had ever committed robbery

Predictor	B	S.E.	Wald	Exp(B)
Public assistance recipient	.007	.212	.001	1.008
Male	1.509	.338	19.887***	4.522
Nonwhite	-.146	.211	.480	.864
Age	-.019	.080	.059	.981
Perceived neighborhood incivility	.021	.017	1.487	1.021
Victim of violent threats	.160	.256	.393	1.174
Perceptions of risk index	.270	.099	7.510**	1.310
Likelihood of aggression	-.030	.067	.200	.970
Protective gun carrier	1.033	.220	22.078***	2.808
Differential association index	.088	.125	.493	1.092
Nonsocial reinforcement index	-.236	.121	3.816	.790
Social control index	.249	.117	4.499*	1.283
Strain index	-.252	.118	4.561*	.777
Gang member	.458	.215	4.518*	1.581
Constant	-3.008			
Chi-Square	185.441***			
-2 Log Likelihood	658.677			
Nagelkerke R^2	.333			

* p<.05   ** p<.01   *** p<.001

CHAPTER 8

Gun Violence Among Young People: What Have We Learned? What Can We Do?

Many explanations have been offered to explain the problem of firearm violence and its role in the larger picture of violence among young people in the United States. We have added to the literature in this area by confirming earlier findings that suggest that firearm possession and use among youths, particularly youths regularly involved in criminal activities, is widespread and commonplace. This study is unique in that our findings suggest that "protective gun carrying," no matter what the motive of the carrier, is highly correlated with violent activity, even after controlling for a number of known theoretical predictors of violence. A number of aspects of the impact of firearms on violent activity among young people were estimated in this study; thus, the discussion of the findings will be presented in three sections. First, the factors that impact gun usage among juveniles—their sources of acquisition, their preferences in choice of firearm, and their reasons for those choices—will be discussed. Next, we examine whether gun possession serves primarily for protection/defense, as the fear of criminal victimization hypothesis would suggest, or whether protective gun carrying has a "triggering effect," inciting violence among youths when violent activity might otherwise have been avoided. In the final section of this discussion, we consider whether various theoretical predictors of delinquency explain relationships between protective gun carrying and violent delinquency.

Patterns and Explanations of Firearm Acquisition and Preferences among Adolescents

This study afforded a rare opportunity to examine the sources of and reasons for adolescent firearm possession among a sample of incarcerated youths. This effort replicated and extended that of Sheley and Wright (1995) whose work serves as the seminal piece in this area. Thus, we used many of the same indicators and variables that demonstrated an association with gun acquisition and use among the respondents in their sample to determine if the relationships uncovered by Sheley and Wright in the early 1990s still held true after the turn of the 21st century. By and large, we confirmed that those relationships prevalent in the 1990s remained in effect today.

We determined that patterns of gun acquisition did not differ dramatically whether we considered responses from the entire sample or restricted our consideration to only those responses of youths who had used a gun in crime. Either way, the two most popular sources of firearm acquisition were to "buy it on the streets" and to "borrow it from a friend or relative." These findings match that of Sheley and Wright ten years earlier. Additionally, as an extension of the work of Sheley and Wright, we estimated a series of contingency analyses to determine what factors (if any) were correlated with the youth's chosen source of firearm acquisition.

We asked the respondents about nine potential sources from which they would consider obtaining a firearm "if they needed to get a gun." Only one of those sources can be considered a "legal" method for acquiring a firearm, and that would only be legal if that youth were an adult. The results indicate that there were no discernible differences among the entire sample in predicting who would choose to obtain a gun from a "gun store." In other words, males were just as likely as females, nonwhites were just as likely as whites, and those youths who had carried a gun for protection and been involved in a wide variety of delinquent activity were just as likely as their counterparts to buy a gun from a gun store if they needed it. Among gun criminals, however, nonwhites were more likely than whites to state that they would purchase a gun from a gun store if they needed it. This finding will be discussed in detail below.

When the sources of firearm acquisition turned to illegal sources, however, the picture changed dramatically. Among the entire sample, the results presented in this study suggest that there were significant differences among those who would consider stealing a gun or buying it illegally (from drug addicts, friends or relatives, cars or houses, stores or shipping trucks, or drug dealers) as a potential means of acquiring a firearm. In practically every case, males, whites, and youths who had (1) carried a gun for protection, (2) engaged in violent activity (e.g., previously committed aggravated assault, robbery, or simple assault or had engaged in a gang fight or used a weapon to commit a crime), or (3) used or sold drugs, were significantly more likely to consider stealing or buying a gun illegally than their counterpart.

When the sample is restricted to gun criminals, however, the impact of these variables is not nearly as dramatic. Among gun criminals, the results presented in this study still suggest that in practically every case, males, Whites, and youths who had sold or used drugs other than marijuana were significantly more likely to consider stealing or buying a gun illegally than their counterpart. For the rest of the relationships, however, the results were inconsistent. Nevertheless, the results suggest that the type of gun the gun criminal used in crime had little to do with the source of gun acquisition, indicating that the cognitive process involved in the determination of which type of gun to use in crime is different than the process involved in the source of gun acquisition. Interestingly, gang membership and whether the individual had been involved in a gang fight, variables often associated with practically all illegal activity, had very little to do with the source of gun acquisition in this sample. With the exception of robbery, which had a significant impact on some of the sources of gun acquisition, engagement in violent activity in general had very little impact on the source of gun acquisition among gun criminals.

Thus, while the results from this study generally support the previous research, our results also provide some revealing findings heretofore undiscovered as well. The most glaring contradiction between the findings from this study and those of other studies involves the relationship between race and source of gun acquisition. As reviewed previously, when a relationship between illegal gun activity and race is uncovered, nonwhites generally are significantly more likely to be involved in that illegal activity than whites. We find the exact opposite in this study; whites are significantly more likely to obtain guns by theft than nonwhites, whether using the entire sample or the subsample of gun criminals. This finding deserves further explanation.

There are two possible explanations for the finding that whites are significantly more likely than nonwhites to obtain guns from illegal sources. First, and most likely, in our opinion, this divergent finding may be due to the sample under study here. By nature of their incarceration, the youths under study here have all had previous involvement with criminal justice authorities and may be considered to be "the worst of the worst" youthful offenders in Indiana. Thus, it could be that those factors that interact with race outside of a correctional facility to explain racial differences in crime (e.g., poverty, disrupted families, criminogenic neighborhoods) are "naturally controlled" in this sample. As such, this finding directly contradicts those who argue that a subculture of violence exists among many nonwhite populations (Wolfgang and Ferracuti 1967) and suggests that, given equal opportunities and limitations, whites are as likely as or more likely than nonwhites to engage in criminal activity.

The second explanation revolves around the responses to the question about using a "legitimate" gun store as a source of gun acquisition in this study. While this argument is purely speculation on our part, the fact that nonwhites were significantly more likely than whites to respond they would buy a gun from a gun store lends credence to that argument that white respondents in this sample may be less likely than nonwhites to know of "gray market" sources of guns-- legitimate gun dealers who might sell a gun to a "straw" purchaser, or a legal gun buyer who will purchase guns for those not legally qualified to buy a gun (Kleck 1991). Thus, whites may be more likely than nonwhites to steal guns because they are not aware of other "quasi-legitimate" sources of guns of which nonwhites in this sample may be aware.

Our findings also concur with those of Sheley and Wright (1995) that those involved in drug distribution and use, particularly distribution and use of "hard" drugs (those other than marijuana), are more likely to carry guns for protection and be willing to commit crimes to obtain firearms. As Sheley and Wright

(1995) suggest, firearms are a prevalent part of the "hard" drug trade; those youths who distribute these drugs often feel they need a gun for protection from their competition or unwilling customers and are willing to go to any means to obtain that gun. Thus, despite the fact that many argue the "crack wars" of the 1980s are over, serious drug distributors still appear to be willing to commit crimes to get guns to assist them in their trade.

Furthermore, the gun criminals in this sample do not appear to differentiate the source of acquisition from the type of gun used; this supports the argument made by Sheley and Wright (1995) that gun criminals (while often selective in their choice of firearm) do not base that choice on the method of acquisition of firearms. This leads us to believe that the youths in this sample realize that obtaining a certain type of gun does not pose much problem for them; if they want a semiautomatic firearm (or a large-caliber or small-caliber firearm, for that matter), they know where they can get one and thus their choice of source of firearm acquisition is not contingent upon their firearm preference.

We were also able to examine the prevalence of firearm possession and use in this sample, what type of guns the juveniles preferred, and the reasons for those preferences. Youths in this sample were quite familiar with guns and many had used guns in crimes. Respondents were in widespread agreement that handguns were far more preferable "tools" than shotguns or rifles. Over half of the sample stated that they had used a handgun in crime compared to less than one in ten who had used a shotgun or an automatic or semiautomatic weapon and less than one in fifty had used a rifle in crime. As Sheley and Wright (1995) suggest, the idea that youths prefer automatic or semiautomatic firearms for use in crime is not supported by the voices of the youths making those choices.

We found few factors that helped us determine why the youths would select one type of gun over another for use in crime. Among the full sample of respondents, race, public assistance, and previous victimization experiences did not have a significant impact on whether a respondent had used a particular type of gun in crime. Every other variable we considered, however, was significantly related to the choice of gun, regardless of the type of gun. Thus, males and those youths who had committed robbery, simple assault, aggravated assault, carried a gun for protection, been involved in a gang fight, used a weapon to commit a crime, been a gang member, and sold or used marijuana or drugs other than marijuana were all significantly more likely to have used each of the types of guns in question than their counterparts.

When we looked only at the subsample of youths who have used a gun to commit a crime in the past, the distinctions become clearer but less consistent. Males are more likely to have used large-caliber handguns than females among those youths who have used guns to commit crimes. Those gun criminals who sold marijuana and were gang members were more likely to have used a medium-caliber handgun to commit crimes than those who had not sold marijuana. Finally, those who sold drugs other than marijuana, gang members, and those who had committed robbery in the past were more likely to have used a small-caliber handgun in the commission of a crime.

Thus, our findings regarding the preference for type of guns generally suggest that using a gun in crime is largely the "master predictor" of the choice of a gun in crime. In other words, those who engage in the illegal activities considered here are significantly more likely to have used *every* type of gun in crime. Once that distinction is made, and we try to determine what predicts the choice of gun among gun criminals, it is much less likely that a choice of a gun is dependent on the other criminal activities considered here. The only consistent pattern that we were able to uncover further supports a finding discussed earlier regarding the culture of hard drug distribution. Among the sample of gun criminals, hard drug distribution appears to be intertwined closely with gang membership and the choice of a small-caliber handgun for use in crime. This choice follows from the fact that those individuals who engage in drug distribution (perhaps even as part of their gang membership) would be more likely to carry firearms and would also be more likely to use those firearms in a transaction where they took either drugs or money by force from someone else. Intuitively, then, if one is more likely to engage in those activities regularly, that individual would be more likely to use a small-caliber handgun in crime, as they are typically easily concealable, inexpensive, and easily replaceable—all the characteristics of the "throwaway gun" commonly referred to in television and other media accounts of crime. Interestingly, these factors had little to do with whether the youths had used shotguns, rifles, or large-caliber guns in crime, those guns most likely to cause serious devastation and most commonly portrayed by the media as rampant among drug dealers. Once again, our findings support those of Sheley and Wright (1995) regarding choice of armament as well.

The results of our examination of why youths choose the guns they do are also strikingly similar to those of Sheley and Wright (1995). Our findings converge with theirs regarding reasons for using a firearm in crime because protection was mentioned by nine in ten respondents who had used a gun in crime as a reason why they chose to use a weapon in crime. The vast majority of the gun criminals felt that a weapon would protect them if they had to defend themselves or if the victim was armed. Although self-protection was listed by the vast majority of the gun criminals as a reason for using a weapon in crime, most also felt that the weapon made them more likely to be successful as well, as most agreed that they might need the weapon to escape a situation and people wouldn't mess with them if they had a weapon. Status among friends had very little to do with why the respondents in this sample chose to use a weapon in crime.

We also conducted a number of contingency analyses for both the entire sample and the subsample of gun criminals in an attempt to isolate the factors that might distinguish between the reasons for using a gun in crime. As with the type of gun chosen, our findings suggest that those who engage in the illegal activities considered here are significantly more likely to state that each of the reasons considered here is an important reason to use a weapon in crime than their counterparts when all respondents are considered. When the subsample of gun criminals is considered, those who sold drugs (both marijuana and drugs other than marijuana) were significantly more likely to carry a gun because the victim might be armed while those who sold drugs other than marijuana were significantly more likely to indicate they carried a weapon because the "victim would not put up a fight," they might "need a weapon to escape from a situation," and they needed a weapon "to insure success in completion of their crime" as well. None of the other variables explained more than one reason for using a weapon in the commission of a crime.

Thus, while our earlier results seem to suggest that guns are an important part of the culture surrounding distribution of drugs other than marijuana, the findings regarding why gun criminals chose to carry guns suggest that those who sold drugs in the sample of gun criminals were significantly different regarding their reasons for carrying guns than their counterparts; they were significantly more likely to indicate they used weapons in crime for both protection and aggression. More will be said about this finding below.

In sum then, our findings regarding the sources of gun acquisition, type of gun preferences, and reasons for use in crime closely mirror those of Sheley and Wright (1995). We do find evidence of a subsample of gun criminals that are somewhat more deviant than their counterparts: those who distribute drugs other than marijuana. While guns are a prevalent part of most of the respondents' lives, those who distribute drugs other than marijuana appear to be markedly different than their counterparts regarding the issue of guns.

Thus, as Sheley and Wright also found, those who distribute drugs other than marijuana and who "also committed predatory crimes exceeded nonpredator counterparts in involvement in most forms of gun activity" (Sheley and Wright 1995, 91). Even among incarcerated youths, it appears that a certain subgroup of respondents is more involved than their counterparts when it comes to drugs and violence.

Gun Possession: Protection or Aggression?

In addition to replicating and extending the work of Sheley and Wright (1995), another purpose of this study was to provide clarification regarding whether youths who regularly carry guns do so for protection or as part of a lifestyle of aggression. The results reviewed earlier suggest that the gun criminals under study here admitted that they used a gun in crime for two reasons: to protect themselves from harm and to increase their chances of a successful criminal transaction.

As such, in chapter six we attempted to disentangle the impact of protective gun carrying on violent activity. We determined that, among this sample of incarcerated adolescents, there were few demographic differences in either firearm possession or violent activity. Those who received public assistance were no more likely to carry firearms or engage in violent activity than; older youths were significantly more likely to carry firearms for protection but were no more likely to engage in violence or robbery. Males were significantly more likely to carry firearms for protection and engage in robbery, but were not significantly more likely to engage in violent activity in general. Additionally, nonwhites were more likely to have carried a gun for protection but were no more likely to have engaged in violent activity or robbery. The lack of significant differences based on demographic factors is probably due to the nature of the sample under study, in that the vast majority of the respondents had engaged in at least one of the violent activities and many had carried firearms regularly.

Nevertheless, the contextual variables did a much better job of distinguishing which youths were more likely to carry guns and engage in violent activities. Gang members were significantly more likely to carry guns for protection, engage in violent activity, and commit robbery than their counterparts. Additionally, those who perceived themselves most at risk of criminal victimization and those from criminogenic neighborhoods were more likely to carry a gun for protection and commit robbery. Victims of violent threats were more likely to have engaged in violent activity.

As such, these findings lend partial support for the fear of criminal victimization hypothesis. Youths from criminogenic neighborhoods and youths who perceive themselves most at risk are most likely to carry firearms for protection. Nevertheless, the examination of violent activities and robbery tends to suggest that protective gun carrying may have a triggering effect for violent activity. Protective gun carriers were significantly more likely to engage in violent activity and to have committed robbery. This association remained even after controlling for the respondent's tendency toward aggressive behavior.

These findings support those alluded to earlier. It appears that protective gun possession has a "triggering" effect on violent behavior. While the youths may originally carry a gun for protection due to the criminogenic environment where they reside and their increased levels of perceived risk, these protective gun carriers are far more likely to engage in both robbery and violent activity in general than their counterparts who do not carry guns for protection.

The cross-sectional nature of this sample does not allow us to make any causal statements regarding whether the protective gun carriers were more likely to engage in violent activity before or as a result of the presence of the gun. Nevertheless, intuitively, we believe that these behaviors occur concurrently. In other words, a criminogenic environment and increased levels of risk may (a) make an individual more likely to engage in violence and (b) make that individual more likely to carry a firearm for protection from the violence that he or she is regularly engaged. It appears then, that carrying a gun for protection and engaging in violent activity are part of a lifestyle and context for some adolescents, making it hard to separate one from the other.

Theoretical Explanations of Protective Gun Carrying and Violent Activity

We then turned to an examination of the relationship of the explanatory ability of four known theoretical predictors of delinquency on protective gun carrying and its subsequent association with violent activity. We tested this relationship using measures from strain theory, differential association theory, social control theory, and nonsocial reinforcement theory. While by no means a definitive test of any of these theoretical perspectives, we felt it was important to determine if the association between protective gun carrying and violent activity could be explained by those theoretical perspectives.

The inclusion of the theoretical measures did not mediate the relationships uncovered above. In other words, males, gang members, youths who perceived themselves most at risk, youths from criminogenic neighborhoods, and protective gun carriers were more likely (and in practically all cases, significantly more likely) to have committed a crime with a gun, to have engaged in violent activity in general, and to have committed robbery. The inclusion of the theoretical perspectives further clarified that these youths were engaging in these violent activities primarily because of their association with delinquent peers (a significant predictor of whether they had committed a crime with a gun and whether they had committed violent activity in general). Additionally, those youths that received the greatest amounts of nonsocial reinforcement from engaging in risky behavior were more likely to carry guns for protection. Interestingly, differential association theory was the only theoretical perspective that had a significant relationship with both violent activity and using a gun in crime. Thus, those youths least attached to school and experiencing the most strain were significantly more likely to have engaged in robbery in their lifetime.

As such, robbery appears to have a different etiology than either using a gun in crime or engaging in violent delinquency in general. It may be those youths who commit robbery are a distinctively different group than their counterparts who engage in violence in general or carry guns for protection. Those youths who carry guns for protection seem to be driven by the intrinsic gratification (nonsocial reinforcement) they receive from engaging in risky behavior, even after controlling for their environment and their demographic variables. Furthermore, robbery seems to also be predicted by poor attachment to school and perceptions of blocked life opportunities. Engaging in violence in general and using a gun in crime, on the other hand, seem to be more dependent on one's peers and the deviant attitudes of those peers.

Even more importantly, the inclusion of the theoretical predictors provides strong support for the triggering effect when it comes to the relationship between protective gun carrying and violent activity. Protective gun carriers remained far more likely to have used a gun in crime, to have engaged in violent activity, and to have committed robbery. These relationships could not be explained by some of the more popular theoretical perspectives from criminological research.

The cross-sectional nature of this study does not allow us to examine temporal effects. As May (2001a) has suggested, it appears that a social milieu exists that encourages protective gun carrying. This social milieu begins with males from criminogenic neighborhoods. From that origin, there are two possible pathways from criminogenic neighborhoods to the protective gun carrying/elevated perceptions of risk/violent activity lifestyle that may be produced.

The first pathway is what we call the "triggering pathway". On this pathway, these youths, in reaction to the perceived growing crime and subsequent risk of criminal victimization in their neighborhoods, engage in protective firearm carrying. Because of the heightened confidence they feel, these youths then expose themselves to situations (including gang membership) that not only heighten their chance of criminal victimization, but also increase their opportunity to engage in other violent delinquent acts as well.

The second pathway is entitled the "delinquent existence" pathway. On this pathway, these youths from criminogenic neighborhoods engage in a series of delinquent activities, three of which include gang membership, firearm possession, and violent activity. Because these youths are surrounded by violence, guns, and victimization, they realize that they have a higher risk of criminal victimization. As such, their heightened perceptions of risk of victimization are not due to their fear or victimization, but a tendency toward delinquency in general. They realize that a risk of victimization is simply one part of their delinquent existence and gun carrying is a necessary "tool" they need for their trade. It is apparent, then, that regardless of the pathway chosen, the end result is the same.

Limitations of the Study

There are three major limitations to this study. The first limitation concerns the cross-sectional nature of the data used in this study. To fully examine the ideas explored in this study, longitudinal data would have been more appropriate. While we uncovered associations between several variables and protective gun carrying and violent delinquency (e.g., perceptions of risk, perceptions of criminogenic neighborhoods, theoretical perspectives), the cross-sectional nature of the data ultimately precluded a definitive statement concerning cause and effect. Longitudinal data are required to rule out any concerns about the temporal ordering of the variables considered in this analysis. Longitudinal data would be particularly helpful in determining the pathway the protective gun carriers navigated to arrive at their destination, a destination at which (at least prior to their incarceration) they regularly carry guns for protection, engage in violent activity, and realize they are at greater risk for criminal victimization than their counterparts who are not in the same life situation.

Another limitation of this study concerns the sample used. As the sample consisted entirely of incarcerated male and female youths in Indiana, the results of this study may not be generalizable to either incarcerated youth populations elsewhere or to the much larger population of nonincarcerated youths. As such, the findings presented here may exaggerate the involvement of youths with firearms and violent forms of offending. Of note, compare the less than 20% lifetime prevalence rate of firearm carrying among nonincarcerated samples in the literature review to the 47% lifetime ownership rate and 40% lifetime protective firearm carrying prevalence rate here.

Nevertheless, the findings presented here mirror those of other studies using incarcerated youths and youths from high-risk groups. Thus, as suggested earlier, those youths who are most familiar with firearms and most involved in delinquency would be more likely to have committed activities that caused them to be incarcerated, and, as such, the fact that these were incarcerated youths may be a latent benefit rather than a limitation.

A third limitation concerns the interaction between the items on the survey and the setting in which the data for this study were collected. For instance, the measure representing perceptions of neighborhood incivility referred to the neighborhood in which they lived prior to incarceration while the perceived risk measure referred to their chances of being victimized in the next year (with no control for how much of that next year would be spent incarcerated). As such, it could be that the associations between those variables and firearm and violent activities uncovered in this study were confounded by the difficulty the respondent may have experienced in making that distinction. Future efforts should be clearer in their specificity regarding these issues.

This study contributes to a growing body of knowledge on the deadly phenomena of firearms and violence among adolescents. The results of this study add to what we have learned in prior research, pointing to the following conclusion: many young people who take precautions to protect themselves from danger and (either as a result of or a precursor to) violence often place themselves at greater risk for both criminal victimization and criminal participation. Thus, as May (2001) suggests, a paradox exists among young people in criminogenic neighborhoods: taking steps to protect oneself from victimization by crime often coincides with putting that individual at risk of greater involvement in crime.

Future studies should use longitudinal data to attempt to unravel the temporal order of this relationship between criminogenic environments, firearm possession, and violent delinquency. By doing so, researchers should be able to more clearly specify the pathway to violence (whether it be the triggering pathway or the delinquent existence pathway) and thus develop intervening steps to dissuade and deter youths from reaching what is often its bitter end: death or prison.

Implications

The results from this study have a number of important policy implications. The results presented here suggest that firearm possession for protection, criminogenic environments, elevated levels of perceived risk, and gang membership have statistically significant associations with violent delinquency. As such, one of the primary focuses of efforts to reduce violence among adolescents must begin with the first step in the pathway to violence: encouraging healthy development for youths in criminogenic neighborhoods. We concur with Wilkinson (2003) that violence prevention efforts begin with a comprehensive strategy that targets "multiple sources of influence on youths" (259) and utilizes a wide range of strategies and resources from a number of different arenas (social, psychological, governmental, and economic).

Of the programs that have been implemented, evaluated, and have demonstrated potential for changing the nature and organization of a neighborhood, they all share the fact that they build the "collective efficacy" of a neighborhood. Whether it is community policing, mentoring, or after-school programs designed to empower the youths in the community and cause them to "give back" to their neighborhood, it is important that these works continue to be implemented in an effort to transform the first "turn" in both pathways presented here: the criminogenic neighborhood.

The second policy implication deals directly with the relationship between firearms among adolescents and violent delinquency. No matter what the origin of adolescent protective firearm possession, it is clear that firearm possession is highly correlated with violent activity. Thus, any effort that removes firearms from the adolescent population should reduce the amount of involvement in violence (if only by removing the potential for greater damage with firearms than other weapons).

Nevertheless, the results presented here mirror those of numerous previous studies that firearms are readily available to those young people who would like to have one. The quantitative and qualitative evidence presented here suggests that, at the beginning of the 21st century, cost is not a deterrent when it comes to adolescent firearm possession. A .25 or .380 caliber pistol, while inexpensive (and, in at least one case, obtained by swapping a pager for it), can provide the protection that youths are seeking from others in their environment and can serve to empower those youths to trigger them to further violence as well.

Cook, Moore, and Braga (2002) outline a number of strategies to:

> develop and evaluate specific gun-control measures that can reduce
> gun crime, suicides, and accidents, while preserving as much legitimate
> use of guns as possible. There is no reason to believe that there is a
> single best policy. Rather, we are looking for a portfolio of policies
> that reflects the full array of gun 'problems.' To some extent this portfolio
> should differ according to local circumstances and values. (325)

Cook et al. (2002) then offer a number of suggestions for reducing gun violence in the United States and categorize these suggestions into federal, state, and local level efforts. As we have stated before, we feel many of their suggestions will be minimally effective in reducing gun violence among youths (e.g., federal legislation to raise the tax on guns and ammunition; requiring all gun transfers to go through federally licensed dealers). By the fact that the vast majority of these youths cannot legally purchase a firearm because of their minor status, any transaction in which they acquire a firearm is, by necessity, an illegal transaction. As such, any measure dealing with monitoring legal gun markets more closely will probably have minimal impact among those youths who are on the pathway to violence presented here.

Nevertheless, Cook et al. (2002) do offer a number of suggestions that could help reduce the flow of firearms through the criminogenic environments in which these youths operate. The first suggestion is to increase cooperation between federal, state, and local law enforcement agents to investigate and prosecute "those who deal in stolen guns and those who engage in illegal gun trafficking" (326). These agencies should use tracing and ballistic imaging recently developed to uncover and punish those who provide weapons to juveniles and strengthen criminal penalties for those who transfer handguns to juveniles. As May (2001) suggests, it is doubtful the change in punishment would reduce adolescent gun violence immediately; nevertheless, if we could reduce the number of these dealers over time, it could potentially reduce firearm availability among adolescents in the future.

Cook et al. (2002) also argue that local law enforcement efforts can be effective as well. They argue, however, that the goal of these policies should not be to simply reduce the availability of guns but to "find other, less costly means that people can use to produce security and reduce fear" (328). These goals can be achieved through a community policing framework; in that framework, law enforcement agencies can mobilize citizens to build that "collective efficacy" described earlier, and increase police-citizen communications to help law enforcement identify those youths and dealers who are involved in the illegal firearm trade.

Finally, Cook et al. (2002) suggest that targeted deterrence efforts, such as Operation Ceasefire in Boston (U.S. Department of Justice 2000b) that combine the efforts of school officials, court officials, law enforcement officers, and juvenile probation officers to (1) reduce gun carrying by offenders on streets; (2) reduce youth involvement and use of firearms; and (3) keep guns out of places where violence is likely to occur, such as homes with a history of domestic violence and rowdy bars or other "hot spots" should be replicated and put into place throughout the country.

The roles gang membership and deviant peers are also important. As those youths whose friends have deviant attitudes and who are gang members are more likely to carry guns for protection and engage in subsequent violent activity, education programs that teach techniques to offset the negative influence of peers may be particularly suitable for reducing protective gun ownership, and subsequent violence, among boys

Each of these efforts described above are important to accomplish two key goals that should reduce protective gun carrying among those youths who would consider it. First, reducing the amount of illegal firearms in the community through identification and prosecution of those who provide guns to adolescents illegally would reduce the ease with which these youths can obtain a firearm (and perhaps increase the costs) by reducing the amount of firearms they can "buy off the streets" or "borrow from a friend or relative." In turn, this should reduce the "need" for protective gun carrying among those who are tangentially involved in violent activities and subsequently reduce the amount of firearm violence even more.

Finally, the evidence suggests that what we have attempted at the end of the 20th century in the United States appears to be working. Violent crime (and firearm-related activities) among youths declined throughout the 1990s and has not increased markedly since. Thus, there is hope that some of the measures currently in place will continue to work in the future. Further exploration, and continued expectations and accountability for reducing gun violence, are not only advisable, but are also essential. Until the United States does not lose a single youth to firearm violence, we haven't achieved our goal.

APPENDIX

Indiana Youth Survey 2001

Researchers from the School of Public and Environmental Affairs at Indiana University-Purdue University Indianapolis (IUPUI) are conducting this survey to determine what teenagers think about such things as recreational activities, peer pressure, risk-taking behavior, drug and alcohol use, and the police. Information such as this will be used to help youth in the state receive better services, counseling, and assistance for many different things.

Your participation in this study is *completely voluntary*. If you agree to take part, you may answer any or all of the questions and you may quit at any time. Please answer the questions honestly. This is not a test—**there are no right or wrong answers.** Your answers on this questionnaire will remain *confidential*. **Do not write your name or any other identifying information on your survey.** All surveys will be destroyed by December 2002.

Please follow the directions given. Make sure your answers are clearly marked. Also, please notice that there are questions on **both sides of the pages**.

QUESTIONS ARE ON BOTH SIDES OF THE PAGES

PLEASE TRY TO WORK QUICKLY WITHOUT SPENDING TOO MUCH TIME ON ANY ONE QUESTION

WE WOULD LIKE TO BEGIN BY ASKING YOU SEVERAL BACK-GROUND QUESTIONS. PLEASE CIRCLE OR FILL IN THE ONE BEST RESPONSE FOR EACH QUESTION.

1. In what year were you born? 19____
          How old are you? _____
2. What is your sex   1. Male   2. Female
3. How do you describe yourself?
          1. African American/Black
          2. White
          3. American Indian
          4. Mexican American/Latino
          5. Asian or Asian American
          6. Other (_____)
4. What was the last grade you were in at school?
          1. 6th 2. 7th 3. 8th 4. 9th 5. 10th 6. 11th 7. 12th
5. Before you were locked up, who were you living with? (**Circle only one**)
          1. Both parents
          2. Mother only
          3. Father only
          4. One parent and a stepparent
          5. One parent and grandparent(s)
          6. Grandparent(s)
          7. Other (_____)
6. Are your natural parents married to each other? Yes   No
7. How many brothers and/or sisters <u>do you have</u>?   _____
8. How many brothers and/or sisters <u>live with you</u>?   _____
9. Approximately how many years have you live at your present address?
     (when you are *not* locked up, that is)
10. Which ONE of the following BEST applies to your father's employment?
     (**Circle only one**)
          1. Takes care of house
          2. Employed full time
          3. Employed part time
          4. Retired
          5. Unemployed but looking for work
          6. Other (_____)
11. What kind of work does/did your father do? _____

12. What is the highest level of schooling your father completed? (**Circle only one**)
    1. 8th grade or less
    2. Some high school
    3. Completed high school
    4. Some College
    5. Completed college
    6. Graduate or professional school after college
    7. Other (_____)
    8. I don't know
13. Which ONE of the following BEST applies to your mother's employment? (**Circle only one**)
    1. Takes care of house
    2. Employed full time
    3. Employed part time
    4. Retired
    5. Unemployed but looking for work
    6. Other (_____)
14. What kind of work does/did your mother do?_____
15. What is the highest level of schooling your mother completed? (**Circle only one**)
    1. 8th grade or less
    2. Some high school
    3. Completed high school
    4. Some College
    5. Completed college
    6. Graduate or professional school after college
    7. Other (_____)
    8. I don't know
16. In the past year, has your family received some form of public assistance (such as WIC, AFDC/welfare, or food stamps)?   1. Yes 2. No
17. What is your religion?
    1. Baptist
    2. Methodist
    3. Presbyterian
    4. Church of Christ
    5. Episcopal
    6. Catholic
    7. Jewish
    8. Other_____

18. How important is religion in your life?
    1. Not important
    2. A little important
    3. Pretty important
    4. Very important
19. <u>Before you were locked up</u>, how often were you going to church?
    1. I didn't go to church
    2. Once or twice a year
    3. A few times each year
    4. Once a month
    5. Every week
    6. More than once each week
    7. Every day
20. Do you have any children?   1. Yes   2. No
21. If so, how many children do you have?   _____
22. Do your children live with you?   1. Yes   2. No

WE WOULD NOW LIKE TO ASK YOU SOME QUESTIONS PERTAINING TO THE TIME *BEFORE YOU GOT LOCKED UP*. FILL IN OR CIRCLE THE ONE BEST RESPONSE FOR EACH QUESTION.

23. Did you have a part-time job? 1. Yes 2. No
24. If yes, how many hours per week did you work?   _____ hours per week
25. During a typical week, about how much money did you have with you to spend? (If you have none, write in 0)
26. During a typical week, about how many evenings do you go out for fun and recreation? (If you don't go out at all, write in a '0')
27. When you were socializing with friends, were there mature adults around who could at least observe you?
28. When you're not locked up, what time do you have to be home *on school nights*? _____
29. When you're not locked up, what time do you have to be home *on weekend nights*?_____
30. On average, how many hours each day did you spend studying or doing homework?_____ hours per day
31. Which ONE of the following best describes your most recent grade average? **(Circle only one)**
    1.A+ 2.A 3.A 4.B+ 5.B 6.B- 7.C+ 8.C 9.C- 10.D or below

32. What is the highest level of school you would like to finish?
    1. 9th grade
    2. 10th grade
    3. 11th grade
    4. High school diploma or GED
    5. Vocational or trade school
    6. Some college
    7. A college degree
33. Honestly, how far do you really think you will get in school?
    1. 9th grade
    2. 10th grade
    3. 11th grade
    4. High school diploma or GED
    5. Vocational or trade school
    6. Some college
    7. A college degree
34. Have you ever been suspended from school? 1. Yes 2. No
    How many times? _____
35. Have you ever been expelled from school? 1. Yes 2. No
    How many times? _____
36. Have you ever had to repeat a grade in school? 1. Yes 2. No
    Which grades? _____

Here are a few things people sometimes consider to be problems in their
local neighborhood. For each item, tell us *how serious* a problem it is in *your*
neighborhood by indicating whether it is:

Not a Problem (1)   Somewhat a Problem (2)   A Very Serious Problem (3)

37. Trash and litter lying around in your neighborhood?
38. Inconsiderate or rowdy neighbors?
39. Graffiti on Sidewalks and walls?
40. Vacant houses or neglected lots?
41. Unsupervised youth?
42. Too much noise
43. People drunk or high on drugs in public?
44. Abandoned cars or car parts lying around?

PLEASE INDICATE WHETHER ANY OF THE FOLLOWING HAVE HAPPENED TO YOU. (1=Yes; 2=No)

45. Had something stolen from me.
46. Had something stolen from me at school.
47. Had someone offer to sell me drugs
48. Had someone offer to sell me drugs at school
49. Had someone threaten to hurt me
50. Had someone threaten to hurt me at school
51. Got into a physical fight
52. Got into a physical fight at school
53. Carried a gun for protection
54. Carried a gun to school for protection
55. Carried a weapon other than a gun for protection
56. Carried a weapon other than a gun to school for protection
57. Hung out with friends for protection
58. Thought about joining a gang for protection
59. Joined a gang for protection
60. Had someone hurt me or threaten to hurt me because of my race
61. Called the police or sheriff because I was afraid of being a victim of a crime
62. Called the police or sheriff because I was a victim of crime

63. What is the <u>most serious</u> punishment that the judge could have given you?
    1. Send me to the Indiana Department of Correction
    2. Waive me to adult court
    3. Send me to an out-of-state placement
    4. Send me to a group home
64. How long have you been here?_____ months
65. How many times have you been locked up?_____
66. Have your probation officer and judge ever talked about waiving you to adult court?   1. Yes   2. No
67. About how many months were you free in the community before being locked up this time: _____ months

Now we would like to ask you about a number of different activities that some people might consider against the law. Remember, your answers are *completely confidential.*

For the activities listed below, we would like to know the number of times you have done any of these things *in the 12 months before you came here* **and then if you have ever done any of these things.**

To answer the questions, just fill in the blanks next to the item. Again, first insert the *number of times* you recall engaging in the activity *in the 12 months before you came here* (if you did not engage in the activity, put a "0" in the blank); then check either "Yes" or "No" to indicate if you have *ever* engaged in the activity.

68. Smoked a pack of cigarettes in one day?
69. Skipped school without an excuse?
70. Been drunk in a public place?
71. Avoided paying for such things as movies, bus rides, or food?
72. Been suspended from school?
73. Bought liquor?
74. Failed to return extra change that a cashier gave to you by mistake?
75. Been loud, rowdy, or unruly in a public place?
76. Hitchhiked where it was illegal to do so?
77. Begged for money or things from strangers?
78. Damaged a car but did not try to notify the owner?
79. Gambled illegally such as betting on sporting events or card playing?
80. Been paid for having sexual relations with someone?
81. Drove a car while drunk?
82. Been a passenger in a car with a drunk driver?
83. Made obscene telephone calls such as calling someone and saying dirty things?
84. Been involved in a gang fight?
85. Sold marijuana or hashish ("pot," "grass," or "hash")
86. Sold hard drugs such as heroin, cocaine, or LSD?
87. Knowingly bought, sold, or held something stolen?
88. Taken a vehicle for a ride (drive) without the owner's permission?
89. Thrown objects (such as rocks, snowballs, or bottles) at cars or people?
90. Stole or tried to steal things worth $5 or less at school?
91. Stole or tried to steal things worth between $5 and $50 at school?
92. Stole or tried to steal things worth more than $50 at school?
93. Stole or tried to steal things worth $5 or less at places other than school?
94. Stole or tried to steal things worth between $5 and $50 at places other than school?
95. Stole or tried to steal things worth more than $50 at places other than school?
96. Carried a hidden weapon other than a plain pocket knife?
97. Purposely damaged/destroyed property belonging to your family members?
98. Purposely damaged/destroyed property belonging to your school?
99. Purposely damaged or destroyed property that did not belong to you (not counting family or school property)?

100. Broken into a building or vehicle (or tried to break in) to steal something or just look around

101. Stole or tried to steal a motor vehicle, such as a car or motorcycle?

102. Used force (strong-arm methods) to get money or things from family members?

103. Used force (strong-arm methods) to get money or things from schoolmates?

104. Used force (strong-arm methods) to get money or things from people other than family members or schoolmates?

105. Hit or threatened to hit a schoolmate or teacher at school?

106. Hit or threatened to hit a family member?

107. Hit or threatened to hit someone other than a schoolmate, teacher, or family member?

108. Attacked someone with the idea of seriously hurting or killing him/her?

109. Had or tried to have sexual relations with someone against their will?

110. Copied/recorded CD's, video tapes, or computer software without permission?

111. Loaded a program on a computer that you or someone else had copied illegally?

112. Had alcoholic beverages (beer, wine, hard liquor)?

113. Had marijuana or hashish ("grass," "pot," "Hash")?

114. Had hallucinogens ("PCP," "LSD," "Acid," "Mushrooms," "Peyote")?

115. Had amphetamines ("Uppers," "Speed")?

116. Had barbiturates ("Downers," "Reds")?

117. Had heroin ("Horse," "Smack")?

118. Had cocaine ("Coke")?

119. Had "crack"?

120. In the past 12 months, how many of your closest friends have done something that they could have gotten arrested for?   ____

121. In the past 12 months, how many of your family members/relatives have done something that they could have gotten arrested for? ____

122. Are you currently a member of a street or youth gang? 1. Yes 2. No

123. Have you ever been a member of a street or youth gang? 1. Yes 2. No

124. Have you ever been asked to join a street or youth gang? 1. Yes 2. No

125. Would you ever consider joining a gang? 1. Yes 2. No

GANG SECTION: IF YOU *HAVE EVER BEEN A MEMBER OF A STREET OR YOUTH GANG*, ANSWER THE FOLLOWING QUESTIONS: (OTHERWISE SKIP DOWN TO THE GUN SECTION)

126. How long were you or have you been a member of a street or youth gang?
     _____ years *and/or*_____ months
127. Why did you join a street or youth gang?   (**Circle all that apply**)
     1.   Protection
     2.   Respect
     3.   Friends are members
     4.   Relatives are members
     5.   Other_____
     6.   Have not joined a gang
128. Do members of your gang <u>SELL</u> drugs?   1. Yes   2. No
129. Do members of your gang <u>USE</u> drugs?   1. Yes   2. No
130. Do members of your gang do things that they could be arrested for (other than sell or use drugs)?   1. Yes   2. No
131. Do you have relatives who are members of a street or youth gang?
                    1. Yes   2. No
132. Do you have friends who are members of a street or youth gang?
                    1. Yes   2. No

GUN SECTION:

133. If I needed to get a gun, I would get one by (**check all that apply**):
     _____Buy it from a gun store
     _____Steal if from a car or house
     _____Steal it from a store or shipping truck
     _____Steal/buy one from a drug addict
     _____Steal/buy it from a drug dealer
     _____Borrow one from a friend or relative
     _____Steal/buy it from a friend or relative
     _____Buy it on the streets
     _____Other (please indicate how_____)
134. How many guns have you ever owned? *number*: _____
135. How many guns have you ever bought? *number*: _____
136. When you committed crimes in the past, how often were you armed with a gun? (Check only one response)
     _____ Always
     _____ Usually
     _____ Sometimes
     _____ Almost never
     _____Never

137. Before you came to this facility, about how often did you use a gun to commit a crime? (Check only one response)

_____ Almost every day

_____ A few times each month

_____ A few times a year

_____ Only once or twice in my life

_____ Never

138. How old were you the first time you committed a crime with a gun?

_____

139. What kinds of guns have you used to commit crimes with? (**List all of them**)

There are many different reasons why a person like yourself might decide to carry a gun or a weapon other than a gun. For each response below, place the number which most accurately describes why you carry a weapon in the blank beside the statement:

Very Important (1)   Somewhat Important (2)   Not Important (3)

140. If I am planning a crime, there is always a chance a victim might be armed.

141. You have to be ready to defend yourself.

142. If you have a weapon when you commit a crime, your victim doesn't put up a fight and you don't have to hurt them.

143. I feel I might need a weapon to escape from a situation.

144. People just don't mess with you when you have a weapon.

145. In my crowd, if you don't have a gun, people don't respect you.

146. My friends would look down on me if I did not carry a gun.

Now we want you to rate THE CHANCE THAT A SPECIFIC THING WILL HAPPEN TO YOU DURING THE COMING YEAR. On a scale from 1 to 10 where 1 means that it's not at all likely and 10 means its very likely- how LIKELY do you think it is that you will ....

_____ 147. Have someone break into your house while your family is away?

_____ 148. Be raped or sexually assaulted?

_____ 149. Be murdered?

_____ 150. Be attacked by someone with a weapon?

_____ 151. Have something that belongs to you taken from you?

_____ 152. Be robbed or mugged?

USING THE SCALE BELOW, PLEASE INDICATE THE EXTENT TO WHICH YOU AGREE OR DISAGREE WITH THE FOLLOWING STATEMENTS:

Strongly Agree (6)   Agree (5)   Somewhat Agree (4)
Somewhat Disagree (3)   Disagree (2)   Strongly Disagree (1)

153. I expect to be better off financially by this time next year.
154. Some school courses are a waste of my time.
155. Most of my neighbors spend a lot of time keeping their house in good shape.
156. If a close friend of mine committed a crime and spent several years in prison, it would really make my life difficult.
157. I like to test myself every now and then by doing something a little risky.
158. My parents or guardians know who I am with when I am away from home.
159. I feel safe from crime in my neighborhood.
160. It has helped me to be locked up at this facility.
161. If a close family member of mine committed a crime and spent several years in prison, it would really make my life difficult.
162. No matter how hard I work, I will never be given the same opportunities as other kids.
163. The best way to solve an argument is to sit down and talk things out, even if it takes an hour or two.
164. I try to look out for myself first, even if it means making things difficult for other people.
165. My parents encourage me to go to college or technical school after high school.
166. Many people I associate with think it's okay to break the law if you can get away with it.
167. In my neighborhood, people will call the police right away if they think a crime is being committed.
168. My teachers allow me to be creative and artistic.
169. I almost always feel better when I am on the move rather than sitting and thinking.
170. When things get complicated, I tend to quit or withdraw.
171. If breaking the law really doesn't hurt anyone and you can make a quick buck doing it, then it's really not that wrong.
172. In my neighborhood, it's easy to know who belongs and who is a stranger.
173. My judge tries to do what is best for me.
174. I take a positive attitude toward myself.
175. My parents or guardians recognize when I have done something wrong.
176. I have used a weapon to commit a crime.

177. I believe that people like me are treated unfairly when it comes to getting a good job.
178. The police care about the people they are trying to protect.
179. My neighborhood is noisy and the streets always seem to have litter on them.
180. I often act on the spur of the moment without stopping to think.
181. My teachers give me all the help I need.
182. People who commit crimes should be ashamed of themselves.
183. On the whole, I am satisfied with myself.
184. I am afraid of being sexually assaulted.
185. If I had connections, I would be more successful.
186. There are drug dealers in my neighborhood.
187. Some police officers have tried to help me out in the past.
188. Sometimes I feel pressured to leave home.
189. I like to get out and do things more than I like to read or think about things.
190. If I see something in a store that I want, I just buy it.
191. My best friends disapprove of people trying drinks of an alcoholic beverage.
192. I am reliable.
193. My parents or guardians keep a pretty close eye on me.
194. When I have a little extra money, I'm more likely to spend it on something I don't really need than to save it for the future.
195. The judge was right to send me here.
196. I am often in situations where people encourage me to do something that might be illegal.
197. When I do a job, I do it well.
198. It is all right to get around the law if you can get away with it.
199. There are gangs in my neighborhood.
200. Sometimes I will take a risk just for the fun of it.
201. My parents or guardians punish me when they know I have done something wrong.
202. I am afraid of being hurt by others because of my race.
203. Suckers deserve to be taken advantage of.
204. I'm more concerned with what happens to me in the short run than in the long run.
205. If I joined a gang, I would gain respect among my friends.
206. I like school.
207. Over the years, a number of the members in my family have been in trouble with the law.
208. Excitement and adventure are more important to me than peace and security.
209. I feel that I am a person of worth, at least on an equal plane with others.
210. It is difficult to get police officers to help people in my neighborhood.

211. Throughout my life, I have had a lot of respect for my mother and father.
212. If someone insulted me, I would be likely to hit or slap them.
213. If I needed to get a gun, I could get one easily.
214. Sometimes I need to lie in order to get a job.
215. I dislike really hard tasks that stretch my abilities to the limit.
216. To get along and be liked, I tend to be what other people expect me to be.
217. I sometimes find it exciting to do things for which I might get in trouble.
218. Society is against people like me.
219. I feel safe when I am out with my friends.
220. Sometimes I feel pressured to help my family with money.
221. I think the police blame certain groups of people for much of the trouble in my neighborhood.
222. Sometimes I will take a risk just for the fun of it.
223. Most of the people I associate with would never break the law.
224. Laws are passed to keep people like me from succeeding.
225. If I took drugs, nothing bad would probably happen to me.
226. I enjoy activities where there is a lot of physical contact.
227. When I get angry, I often stay angry for hours.
228. I am afraid of being attacked by someone with a weapon.
229. Compared to most families, my family is pretty well off.
230. No matter how small the crime, breaking the law is a serious matter.
231. After making a decision, the outcome I expected usually matches the actual outcome.
232. I like to take chances.
233. My parents provide help with my homework when it's needed.
234. If things upset other people, it's their problem, not mine.
235. I am afraid of having my money/possessions taken from me.
236. My best friends disapprove of people taking illegal drugs occasionally.
237. It is frustrating to see people driving nicer cars and living in better homes than I do.
238. I am satisfied with the way my teachers treat me.
239. I'd rather spend my money on something I want now than to put it in the bank.
240. It is morally wrong to break the law.
241. I have often considered joining a gang for protection.
242. Sometimes I rather enjoy going against the rules and doing things that I'm not supposed to do.
243. If I had a choice, I would almost always rather do something physical rather than something mental.
244. There are places at school where I'm afraid to go (i.e., bathroom, cafeteria, gym, etc.) because I might become a victim of a crime.
245. I have as good a chance as other kids of getting a good job when I graduate.
246. When I am really angry, other people better stay away from me.

247. Even with a good education, people like me will have to work harder to make a living.
248. My neighborhood is getting worse and worse all the time.
249. If I took drugs, I most likely would not get caught.
250. I am satisfied with the clothes I have to wear.
251. The things I like to do best are dangerous.
252. I find most of my courses interesting.
253. My parents check on whether I have done my homework.
254. At work it's sometimes necessary to break the rules in order to get ahead.
255. Right now, I'm satisfied with how much money I have to live on.
256. On the whole, cops are honest.
257. I am afraid of being beaten up.
258. I enjoy going on roller coaster rides.
259. I am satisfied with the decisions I get to make concerning my education.
260. Every time I try to get ahead, something or someone stops me.
261. Almost anything can be fixed in the courts if you have enough money.
262. Most of the people living in my neighborhood are good, upstanding citizens.
263. I don't devote much thought and effort to preparing for the future.
264. Sometimes I feel pressured to provide for myself (such as clothes and other things you need).
265. I am afraid of being shot.
266. My chances for making a lot of money in life are not very good.
267. I frequently try to avoid projects that I know will be difficult.
268. When I have a serious disagreement with someone, it is usually hard for me to talk calmly about it without getting upset.
269. Taking things from supermarkets and department stores doesn't hurt anyone.
270. I am satisfied with the amount of spending money I get.
271. I am afraid to go to school because I might become a victim of a crime.
272. Doing well in school is important for getting a good job.
273. Court decisions are almost always just.
274. I believe that there is only one true religion.
275. Through hard work, I can be as successful as I want to be.
276. People who drink large amounts of alcohol are threats to the safety of others.
277. If you are a close friend or relative of someone who is beaten up or wounded in a robbery, that makes you a victim too.
278. My parents or guardians know where I am when I am away from home.
279. I am usually calm and not easily upset.
280. I am trustworthy.
281. In the long run, I expect to be satisfied with how much money I'll have to live on.

282. I am afraid to attend school events (i.e., football games, dances, etc.) because of fights.
283. I would rather associate with people who obey the law than with people who don't.
284. I get to make any important decisions concerning me.
285. I feel safe from crime at my school.
286. A person who does not have enough money to hire a lawyer can still get a fair trial in this state.
287. I wish I could have more respect for myself.
288. Realistically, I don't think I'll make as much money as I'd like.
289. Most individuals who get attacked or robbed on the street should have known better than to be in a place where that could happen.
290. My teachers encourage me to continue my education after high school.
291. If I were thinking of breaking the law, my family would tell me not to do it.
292. I much prefer doing things that pay off right away rather than in the future.
293. If I wanted to get some money for stolen goods, I would know where to go or who to see.
294. I feel I do not have much to be proud of.
295. I can make it at work without having to cheat or lie.
296. Going to school has been an enjoyable experience for me.
297. If I were thinking of breaking the law, my friends would tell me not to do it.
298. The things in life that are easiest to do bring me the most pleasure.
299. I am able to do things as well as most other people.
300. I feel safe from crime in my home.
301. In the long run, I expect to be better off financially than I am.
302. On the whole, judges are honest and kindhearted.
303. By failing to take reasonable precautions, many people whose houses are burglarized have themselves to blame.
304. The things that I learn in school will be important for me later in life.
305. I get angry when I see people who have a lot more money than I do spending their money on foolish things.
306. I rarely need friends' advice to choose movies, books or music.
307. Tests are poor measures of my ability.
308. Sometimes I think I am no good at all.
309. I often do whatever brings me pleasure here and now, even at the cost of some distant goal.
310. I would go out of my way to discourage a friend from using hard drugs.
311. I am satisfied with the amount of money my parent(s) earn.
312. Persons should have the right to use crack or cocaine if they want to, so long as they don't interfere with other people.
313. I am afraid to stay late after school because I might become a victim of a crime.
314. My probation officer tries hard to help me stay out of trouble.

315. What others think of me does not bother me a lot.
316. I've often been frustrated in my efforts to get ahead in life.
317. If I wanted to buy stolen goods at a low price, I would know where to go or who to see.
318. I am afraid to go out at night because I might become a victim of a crime.
319. At least half the things that get people into trouble with the law are beyond their control.
320. Before I do something, I try to consider how my friends will react to it.
321. I feel that I have a number of good qualities.
322. It is often hard for me to go on with my work if nobody encourages me.
323. Many drug laws were designed mainly to keep deprived groups at a disadvantage.
324. I can let people know that I am irritated or angry without losing my temper.
325. Most school work that is given to me is meaningful and important.
326. Most people will never become successful unless they get at least one lucky break.
327. It's okay to lie if it keeps your friends out of trouble.
328. It bothers me that most people have more money to live on than I do.
329. My best friend encourages me to continue my education after high school.
330. When I am angry with someone I often take it out on anybody who happens to be around.
331. What I do today usually can change what might happen to me tomorrow.
332. If I wanted to plan a crime, I know some people who would help me plan it.
333. Sometimes I feel pressured to get a job (if you have a job, did you feel pressured to go to work).
334. If I ever did anything wrong, my family would tell me that they were disappointed.
335. When faced with a problem, I usually look at what sort of outside things in my environment may be adding to the problem.
336. If you want your fellow workers to like you, you may have to cover up for them.
337. People are fools to work for a living if they can get by some easier way, even if it means breaking the law.
338. After I have solved a problem, I spend some time trying to figure out what went right or wrong.
339. I have seen things happen to other people that make me almost sad enough to cry.
340. I am satisfied with the way my parent(s) provide for me.
341. I am often blamed for things that are not my fault.
342. I have the ability to solve most problems, even when at first no solution is obvious.
343. Violating an official government rule or policy is never justified.
344. If the cops don't like you, they will get you for anything.

345. One of the best ways to handle most problems is just not to think about them.
346. Often when I'm angry at people, I feel more like hurting them than talking to them about why I am angry.
347. Most successful people used some illegal means to become successful.
348. I'm not very sympathetic to other people when they are having problems.
349. Advice that I get from my probation officer usually is not worth much.
350. Unexpected interruptions to my daily routine bother me more than they bother most people.
351. Police rarely try to help people.
352. I lose my temper pretty easily.
353. It's okay to cheat when you feel others are being unfair to you.
354. I seem to have more energy and a greater need for activity than most people my age.
355. People should have the right to choose for themselves whether or not to use marijuana.
356. Thinking of similar past problems does not help much when I am trying to solve a new problem
357. My best friends disapprove of people smoking one or more packs of cigarettes per day.
358. My probation officer cares about me as a person.
359. As a rule I have little difficulty in putting myself in other people's shoes, even when I disagree with them.
360. I have to be willing to break some rules if I want to be popular with my friends.
361. I have an organized way to compare choices and make decisions.
362. I have a lot of respect for the police in the community I live in.
363. I feel good about myself when I live up to the expectations my probation officer has for me.
364. Sometimes I get so charged up emotionally that I can't think of many ways of dealing with a problem I face.
365. The high of taking drugs is greater than the risk.
366. I regard my probation officer as a source of help when I have a problem.
367. No matter what I think of them personally, police have such tough jobs to do that they should be paid well for their work.
368. No matter where people come from, they can still get ahead through honest work.
369. I will try to get things I want even when I know it's causing problems for other people.
370. All laws should be strictly obeyed simply because they're laws.
371. Police almost always have a good reason when they stop somebody.
372. I don't like to work on a problem unless I can expect to come out with a clear-cut solution.

373. It's okay for you to take and keep things that people are careless enough to leave laying around.
374. My probation officer doesn't understand my situation very well.
375. It is the duty of a citizen to go along with anything our elected leaders decide to do.

THANK YOU FOR PARTICIPATING IN THIS STUDY

REFERENCES

Agnew, R. 1992. Foundation for a general strain theory of crime and delinquency. *Criminology* 30:47-87.

————. 2001. Building on the foundation of general strain theory: Specifying
the types of strain most likely to lead to crime and delinquency. *Journal of
Research in Crime and Delinquency* 38:319-361.

Agnew, R., Timothy Brezina, J.P. Wright, and F.T. Cullen. 2002. Strain, personality traits, and delinquency: Extending general strain theory. *Criminology* 40:43-72.

Agnew, R., and H.R.White. 1992. An empirical test of general strain theory.
Criminology 30:475-499.

Anderson, R.N. 2002. *Deaths: Leading causes for 2000*. Atlanta: Centers for
Disease Control, National Vital Statistics Report.

Arnett, J. 1995. The young and the reckless: Adolescent reckless behavior. *Current Directions in Psychological Science* 4 (3):67-71.

Arria, A.M., N.P. Wood, and J. Anthony. 1995. Prevalence of carrying a weapon
and related behaviors in urban schoolchildren, 1989 to 1993. *Archives of
Pediatric and Adolescent Medicine* 149:1345-1350.

Arthur, J. A. 1992. Criminal victimization, fear of crime, and handgun ownership among blacks: Evidence from national survey data. *American Journal
of Criminal Justice* 16 (2):121-141.

Ash, P., A.L. Kellerman, D. Fuqua-Whitley, and A. Johnson. 1996. Gun acquisition and use by juvenile offenders. *Journal of the American Medical Association* 275 (22):1754-1758.

Asmussen, K. J. 1992. Weapon possession in public high schools. *School Safety*
28:28-30.

Associated Press. 2003. Kids: Gang ties in New Orleans shooting. *CBS News*,
April 14. http://www.cbsnews.com/stories/2003/04/24/national/
main550894.shtml (accessed May 19, 2005).

————. 2005. High school shooting spree leaves 10 dead. *Fox News*, March 22.
http://www.foxnews.com/story/0,2933,151085,00.html (accessed May 19,
2005).

Bailey, S.L., R.L. Flewelling, and D.P. Rosenbaum. 1997. Characteristics of students who bring weapons to school. *Journal of Adolescent Health* 20:261-270.

Baron, S.W., and T.F. Hartnagel. 1997. Attributions, affect, and crime: Street youths' reactions to unemployment. *Criminology* 35:409-434.

Bergstein, J. M., D. Hemenway, B. Kennedy, S. Quaday, and R. Ander. 1996. Guns in young hands: A survey of urban teenagers' attitudes and behaviors related to handgun violence. *Journal of Trauma, Injury, Infection, and Critical Care* 41 (5):794-798.

Berkowitz, L., and A. LePage. 1967. Weapons as aggression-eliciting stimuli. *Journal of Personality and Social Psychology* 7:202-207.

Birkbeck, C., G. LaFree, L. Gabaldon, A. Bassin, N. Wilson, M. Fernandez, and M. Pacheco. 1999. Controlling New Mexico juveniles' possession and use of firearms. *Justice Research and Policy* 1(1):25-49.

Bjerregaard, B., and A.J. Lizotte. 1995. Gun ownership and gang membership. *Journal of Criminal Law and Criminology* 86 (1):37-58.

Bluhm, J., and D.A. Fahrenthold. 2004. Student slain in school shooting at Ballou. *Washington Post*, February 3.

Blumstein, A. 1995. *Violence by young people: Why the deadly nexus?* Washington, DC: National Institute of Justice.

Brown, Ben. 2004. Juveniles and weapons: Recent research, conceptual considerations, and programmatic interventions. *Youth Violence and Juvenile Justice* 2 (2):161-184.

Butts, J., M. Coggeshall, C. Gouvis, D. Mears, J. Travis, M. Waul, and R. White. 2002. *Youth, guns, and the juvenile justice system.* Washington, DC: Urban Institute.

Callahan, C.M., and F.P. Rivara. 1992. Urban high school youth and handguns: A school-based survey. *Journal of the American Medical Association* 267 (22):3038-3042.

Callahan, C.M., F.P. Rivara, and J.A. Farrow. 1993. Youth in detention and handguns. *Journal of Adolescent Health* 14:350-355.

Cao, L. 2004. *Major criminological theories: Concepts and measurement.* Belmont, CA: Wadsworth.

Cao, L., and X. Deng. 1998. Shoplifting: A test of an integrated model of strain, differential association, and seduction theories. *Sociology of Crime, Law, and Deviance* 1:65-83.

Cella, M. 2004. Youth gun deaths rise; Overall rate dips. *Washington Times*, August 17.

Cernkovich, S.A. 1978. Evaluating two models of delinquency causation: structural theory and control theory. *Criminology* 16:335-352.

Cernkovich, S.A. and P.C. Giordano. 1979. Delinquency, opportunity, and gender. *Journal of Criminal Law and Criminology* 70:145-151.

————. 1979. A comparative analysis of male and female delinquency. *Sociological Quarterly* 20:131-145.

————. 1987. Family relationships and delinquency. *Criminology* 25 (2):295-321.

————. 1992. School bonding, race, and delinquency. *Criminology* 30 (2):261-289.

Cernkovich, S. A., P.C. Giordano, and M.D. Pugh. 1985. Chronic offenders: The missing cases in self-report delinquency research. *Journal of Criminal Law and Criminology* 76 (3):705-732.

Chandler, K.A., C.D. Chapman, M.R. Rand, and B.M. Taylor. 1998. *Students' reports of school crime: 1989 and 1995*. Washington, DC: U.S. Departments of Education and Justice.

Cloward, R.A., and L.E. Ohlin. 1960. *Delinquency and opportunity: A theory of delinquent gangs*. New York: Free Press.

Cohen, A.K. 1955. *Delinquent boys: The culture of the gang*. New York: Free Press.

Cook, P.J., M.H. Moore, & A.B. Braga. 2002. Gun control. In *Crime: Public Policies for Crime Control*, ed. James Q. Wilson and Joan Petersilia, 291-330. Oakland, CA: Institute for Contemporary Studies Press.

Cunningham, P.B., S.W. Henggeler, S.P. Limber, G.B. Melton, and M.A. Nation. 2000. Patterns and correlates of gun ownership among nonmetropolitan and rural middle school students. *Journal of Clinical Child Psychology* 29 (3):432-442.

Durant, R.H., A.G. Getts, C. Cadenhead, and E.R.Woods. 1995. The association between weapon carrying and the use of violence among adolescents living in and around public housing. *Journal of Adolescent Health* 17:376-380.

Durant, R. H., J. Kahn, P.H. Beckford, and E.R.Woods. 1997. The association of weapon carrying and fighting on school property and other health risk and problem behaviors among high school students. *Archives of Pediatric Adolescent Medicine* 151:360-366.

Elliot, D. S., S.S. Ageton, D. Huizinga, B.A. Knowles, and R.J. Canter. 1983. The prevalence and incidence of delinquent behavior: 1976-1980. Boulder, CO: Behavioral Research Institute.

Farrington, D., and R. Loeber. 2000. Epidemiology of juvenile violence. *Child and Adolescent Psychiatric Clinics of North America* 9:733-748.

Federal Bureau of Investigation. 2003. *Crime in the United States- 2002*. Washington, DC.

Ferraro, K. F. 1995. *Fear of crime: Interpreting victimization risk*. Albany, NY: State University of New York Press.

Fingerhut, L.A., and K.K. Christoffel. 2002. Firearm-related death and injury among children and adolescents. *The Future of Children* 12 (2):25-37.

Gibbs, N. 2001. It's only me. *Time* 157 (11):22-24.

Gottfredson, D.C. 2001. *Schools and delinquency.* New York: Cambridge University Press.

Gove, W.R., and C. Wilmoth. 1990. Risk, crime and neurophysiological highs: A consideration of brain processes that may reinforce delinquency and criminal behavior. In *Crime in Biological, Social, and Moral Contexts,* ed. L. Ellis and H. Hoffman. New York: Praeger.

Grasmick, H.G., and R.J. Bursik Jr. 1990. Conscience, significant others, and rational choice: Extending the deterrence model. *Law and Society Review* 24:837-861.

Greenberg, D.F. 1999. The weak strength of social control theory. *Crime and Delinquency* 45 (1):66-82.

Grunbaum, J.A., L. Kann, S.A. Kinchen, B. Williams, J.G. Ross, R. Lowry, and L. Kolbe. 2002. Youth risk behavior surveillance–United States, 2001. *Morbidity and Mortality Weekly Report* 51 (June 28).

Harris, L. 1993. a survey of experiences, perceptions, and apprehensions about guns among young people in america. L.H. Research, Inc., Study 930019.

Hawkins, S.R., A. Campanaro, T.B. Pitts, and H. Steiner. 2002. Weapons in an affluent suburban school. *Journal of School Violence* 1 (1):53-65.

Hemenway, D., D. Prothrow-Stith, J.M. Bergstein, R. Ander, and B.P. Kennedy. 1996. Gun carrying among adolescents. *Law and Contemporary Problems* 59 (1):39-53.

Hirschi, T. 1969. *Causes of delinquency.* Berkeley, CA: University of California Press.

Jarjoura, G.R., and D.C. May. 2000. Integrating criminological theories to explain violent forms of delinquency. *Caribbean Journal of Criminology and Social Psychology* 5 (1,2):81-102.

Johnson, R.E., A.C. Marcos, and S.J. Bahr. 1987. The role of peers in the complex etiology of adolescent drug use. *Criminology* 25:323-339.

Kann, L., S. A. Kinchen, B. I. Williams, J.G. Ross, R. Lowry, J.A. Grunbaum, and Lloyd J. Kolbe. 2000. *Youth Risk Behavior Surveillance-United States, 1999.* Atlanta: Centers for Disease Control.

Kaufman, P., Chen, X., Choy, S. P., Peter, K., Ruddy, S., Miller, A. K., Fleury, J. K., Chandler, K. A., Plany, M. G., & Rand, M. R. (2001). *Indicators of school crime and safety: 2001.* Washington, DC: U.S. Departments of Education and Justice, NCES 2002-113/NCJ-190075. http://nces.ed.gov/pubs2002/crime2001/.

Kingery, P.M., M.B. Coggeshall, and A.A. Alford. 1999. Weapon carrying by youth: Risk factors and prevention. *Education and Urban Society,* 31 (3):309-333.

Kingery, P.M., B.E. Pruitt, and G. Heuberger. 1996. A profile of rural Texas adolescents who carry handguns to school. *Journal of School Health* 66:18-22.

Kleck, G. 1991. *Point Blank.* New York: Aldine de Gruyter.

Knoke, D., G.W. Bohrnstedt, and A. Potter Mee. 2002. *Statistics for social data analysis (4th ed.)*. Belmont, CA: Wadsworth/Thomson Learning.

Krug, E.G., L.L. Dahlberg, and K.E. Powell. 1996. Childhood homicide, suicide, and firearm deaths: An international comparison. *World Health Statistics Quarterly* 49(3-4):230-235.

Kulig, J., J. Valentine, J. Griffith, and R. Ruthazer. 1998. Predictive model of weapon carrying among urban high school students. *Journal of Adolescent Health* 22:312-319.

Limber, S. P. and P.M. Pagliocca. 2000. Firearm possession and use among youth: Reanalysis of findings from a survey of incarcerated youth. http://www.scdps.org/ojp/Reanalysis%20final%20report.pdf.

Lizotte, A. J., D.J. Bordua, and C.S. White. 1981. Firearms ownership for sport and protection: Two not so divergent models. *American Sociological Review* 46:499-503.

Lizotte, A.J., M.D. Krohn, J.C. Howell, K. Tobin, and G.F. Howard 2000. Factors influencing gun carrying among young urban males over the adolescent-young adult life course. *Criminology* 38 (3):811-834.

Lizotte, A.J., and D. Sheppard. 2001. *Gun use by male juveniles: Research and prevention*. Washington, DC: U.S. Department of Justice, Office of Juvenile Justice and Delinquency Prevention, NCJ 188992.

Lizotte, A. J., I.M. Tesoriero, T. P. Thornberry, and M.D. Krohn. 1994. Patterns of adolescent firearm ownership and use. *Justice Quarterly* 11 (1):51-74.

Luster, T., and S.M. Oh. 2001. Correlates of male adolescents carrying handguns among their peers. *Journal of Marriage and Family* 63 (3):714-727.

MacDorman, M.F., A.M. Minino, D.M. Strobino, and B. Guyer. 2002. Annual summary of vital statistics-2001. *Pediatrics* 110(6):1037-1052.

Malecki, C.K., and M.K. Demaray. 2003. Carrying a weapon to school and perceptions of social support in an urban middle school. *Journal of Emotional and Behavioral Disorders* 11 (3):169-178.

Malek, M.K., B. Chang, and T.C. Davis. 1998. Fighting and weapon-carrying among seventh-grade students in Massachusetts and Louisiana. *Journal of Adolescent Health* 2:94-102.

Matsueda, R.L. 1982. Testing control theory and differential association: A causal modeling approach. *American Sociological Review* 47:489-504.

Matsueda, R.L., and K. Heimer. 1987. Race, family structure, and delinquency: A test of differential association and social control theories. *American Sociological Review* 52:826-840.

May, D.C. 1999. Scared kids, unattached kids, or peer pressure: Why do students carry firearms to school? *Youth and Society*, 31(1):100-127

———. 2001a. *Adolescent fear of crime, perceptions of risk, and defensive behaviors: An alternative explanation of delinquency*. Lewiston, NY: Edwin Mellen Press.

————. 2001b. The effect of fear of sexual victimization on adolescent fear of crime. *Sociological Spectrum* 21:141-174.

————. 2003. Nonsocial reinforcement and violence: Can juvenile justice policies be effective against intrinsic gratification received from violent activity among youth? *Journal for Juvenile Justice and Detention Services* 18(1):1-18.

May, D.C., J.D. Nichols, and P.L. Eltzroth. 1998. Risky behaviors among adolescents in the Midwest: Personal gratification or peer pressure. Paper presented at annual meetings of the Midwest Criminal Justice Conference, Chicago.

McNabb, S.J., T.A. Farley, K.E. Powell, H.R. Rolka, and J.M. Horan. 1996. Correlates of gun-carrying among adolescents in south Louisiana. American *Journal of Preventive Medicine* 12(2):96-102.

Merton, R.K. 1938. Social structure and anomie. *American Sociological Review* 3:672-682.

Miller, M.H., F.A. Esbensen, and A. Freng. 1999. Parental attachment, parental supervision and adolescent deviance in intact and non-intact families. *Journal of Crime and Justice* 22(2):1-30.

Moore, S.M., and D.A. Rosenthal. 1993. Venturesomeness, impulsiveness, and risky behavior among older adolescents. *Perceptual and Motor Skills* 76(1):98.

Nye, F.I. 1958. *Family relationships and delinquent behavior.* New York: John Wiley.

Orpinas, P., N. Murray, and S. Kelder. 1999. Parental influences on students' aggressive behaviors and weapon carrying. *Health Education and Behavior* 26(6):774-787.

Pastore, A.L., and K. Maguire, eds. 2003. *Sourcebook of criminal justice statistics.* http://www.albany.edu/sourcebook/ (accessed December 27, 2003).

Rankin, J.H., and R. Kern. 1994. Parental attachments and delinquency. *Criminology* 32(4):495-515.

Reckless, W.C. 1961. A new theory of delinquency and crime. *Federal Probation* 25:42-46.

Reiss, A.J. 1951. Delinquency as the failure of personal and social controls. *American Sociological Review* 16:196-207.

Roth, J. A. 1994. *Firearms and Violence.* U.S. Department of Justice: National Institute of Justice.

Sheley, J. F. 1994a. Drug activity and firearms possession and use by juveniles. *Journal of Drug Issues* 24(3):363-382.

————. 1994b. Drugs and guns among inner-city high school students. *Journal of Drug Education* 24(4):303-321.

Sheley, J. F., and V.E. Brewer. 1995. Possession and carrying of firearms among suburban youth. *Public Health Reports* 110:18-26.

Sheley, J.F., and J.D. Wright. 1993a. *Gun acquisition and possession in selected juvenile samples.* Washington, DC: National Institute of Justice, Office of Juvenile Justice and Delinquency Prevention Research in Brief, NCJ 145326.

———. 1993b. Motivations for gun possession and carrying among serious juvenile offenders. *Behavioral Sciences and the Law* 11(4):375-388.

———. 1995. *In the line of fire: Youth, guns, and violence in urban America.* New York: Aldine de Gruyer.

———. 1998. *High school youths, weapons, and violence: A national survey.* Washington, DC: National Institute of Justice Research in Brief, NCJ 172857.

Simon, T.R., A.E. Crosby, and L.L. Dahlberg. 1999. Students who carry weapons to high school: Comparison with other weapon-carriers. *Journal of Adolescent Health* 24(5):340-348.

Simon, T.R., C.W. Dent, and S. Sussman. 1997. Vulnerability to victimization, concurrent problem behaviors, and peer influence as predictors of in-school weapon carrying among high school students. *Violence and Victims* 12:277-289.

Simon, T.R., J.L. Richardson, C.W. Dent, C. Chou, and B.R. Flay. 1998. Prospective pyschosocial, interpersonal, and behavioral predictors of handgun carrying among adolescents. *American Journal of Public Health* 88(6):960-963.

Simons, R.L., and P.A. Gray. 1989. Perceived blocked opportunity as an explanation of delinquency among lower-class black males: A research note. *Journal of Research in Crime and Delinquency* 26:90-101.

Smith, D. A., and C.D. Uchida. 1988. The social organization of self-help: A study of defensive weapon ownership. *American Sociological Review* 53:94-102.

Smith, M.D. 1996. Sources of firearm acquisition among a sample of inner-city youth: Research results and policy implications. *Journal of Criminal Justice* 24(4):361-367.

Smith, M.D., and J. Sheley. 1995. The possession and carrying of firearms among a sample of inner-city high school females. *Journal of Crime and Justice* 18(1):109-123.

Snyder, H.N. 2001. *Law enforcement and juvenile crime.* Washington, DC: Office of Juvenile Justice and Delinquency Prevention Juvenile, Offenders and Victims National Report Series Bulletin.

Sutherland, E. H. 1947. *Principles of criminology* (4th ed.). Philadelphia: Lippincott.

Sutherland, E. H., and D. Cressey. 1970. *Criminology* (8th ed.). Philadelphia: Lippincott.

Tittle, C.R., M.J. Burke, and E. Jackson. 1986. Modeling Sutherland's theory of differential association: Toward an empirical clarification. *Social Forces* 65:405-432.

U.S. Department of Justice. Office of Juvenile Justice and Delinquency Prevention. 2000. Kids and guns. Washington, DC:, 1999 National Report Series.
———. 2000. National integrated firearms violence reduction strategy. Washington, DC: Department of Justice.

U.S. Department of the Treasury. Bureau of Alcohol, Tobacco, and Firearms. 2002. Crime gun trace reports (2000). Washington, DC.

Vold, G.B., T.J. Bernard, and J.B. Snipes. 1998. *Theoretical criminology* (4th ed.). New York: Oxford University Press.

Vowell, P.R., and D.C. May. 2000. Another look at classic strain theory: receipt of public assistance, perceived blocked opportunity and gang membership as predictors of adolescent violent behavior. *Sociological Inquiry* 70(1):42-60.

Webster, D.W., L.H. Freed, S. Frattorolli, and M.H. Wilson. 2002. How delinquent youths acquire guns: Initial versus most recent gun acquisitions. *Journal of Urban Health* 79(1):60-69.

Webster, D.W., P.S. Gainer, and H.R. Champion. 1993. Weapon carrying among inner-city junior high school students: Defensive behavior vs. aggressive delinquency. *American Journal of Public Health* 83(11):1604-1608.

Wells, W., and J. Horney 2002. Weapon effects and individual intent to do harm: Influences on the escalation of violence. *Criminology* 40:265-296.

Wilcox, P. 2002. Self help? Examining the anti-crime effectiveness of citizen weapon possession. *Sociological Focus* 35:145-167.

Wilcox Rountree, P. 2000. Weapons at school: Are the predictors generalizable across context? *Sociological Spectrum* 20:291-324.

Wilcox, P., and R.R. Clayton. 2001. A multilevel analysis of school-based weapon possession. *Justice Quarterly* 18(3):509-541.

Wilcox, P., D.C. May, and S.L. Roberts. 2004. Student weapon possession and "fear and loathing": Unraveling the temporal order. Paper presented at the annual meetings of the American Society of Criminology, Nashville, TN.

Wilkinson, D. L. 2003. *Guns, violence, and identity among African American and Latino youth.* New York: LFB Scholarly Publishing LLC.

Wilson, J. Q. and R. J. Herrnstein. 1985. *Crime and human nature.* New York: Simon and Schuster, Inc.

Wilson, J. M. and P. A. Zirkel. 1994. When guns come to school. *American School Board Journal* 181:32-34.

Wood, P.B., J.K. Cochran, B. Pfefferbaum, and B.J. Arneklev. 1995. Sensation-seeking and delinquent substance use: An extension of learning theory. *Journal of Drug Issues* 25(1):173-193.

Wood, P.B., W.R. Gove, J.A. Wilson, and J.K. Cochran. 1997. Nonsocial rein-forcement and habitual criminal conduct: An extension of learning theory. *Criminology* 35(2):335-366.

Wolfgang, M. and F. Ferracuti. 1967. *The subculture of violence.* London: Tavistock.

Wright, J.D. and P. H, Rossi. 1986. *Armed and considered dangerous.* New York: Aldine de Gruyter.

Wright, J. D., and L. Marston. 1975. The ownership of the means of destruction: Weapons in the United States. *Social Problems*, 23:92-107.

Wright, J. D., P. Rossi, and K. Daly. 1983. *Under the gun: Weapons, crime, and violence in America.* New York: Aldine.

Wright, J.D., J.F. Sheley, and M.D. Smith. 1992. Kids, guns, and killing fields. *Society*, 30(1):84-89.

Zimring, F.E. and G. Hawkins. 1997. *Crime is not the problem: Lethal violence in America.* Oxford: Oxford University Press.

ABOUT THE AUTHORS

David C. May is an associate professor and Kentucky Center for School Safety Research Fellow in the Department of Correctional and Juvenile Justice Services at Eastern Kentucky University. He has published numerous articles in the areas of causes of juvenile delinquency, firearm possession among youth, and adolescent fear of crime and a book that examines the relationship between adolescent fear of crime and weapon-related delinquency.

G. Roger Jarjoura is an associate professor of criminal justice in the School of Public and Environmental Affairs, Indiana University-Purdue University Indianapolis. He received his Ph.D. in criminology from the University of Maryland. His research and teaching interests focus on the relationship between social class and delinquency, the operations of the juvenile justice system, and the cognitive thought processes of juvenile offenders.